HOW I FIXED MY CHEST FAT

90 DAYS TRANSFORMATION MANUAL

Tarun Gill

Invincible Publishers

First published in India in 2019

ISBN : 978-93-88333-52-8

Invincible Publishers

Registered Address: 201A, SAS Tower, Sector 38, Gurgaon-122003

Printed in India by Excel Printers Pvt. Ltd.

The information in this book is meant to supplement, not replace, proper (name your sport) training. Like any sport involving speed, equipment, balance and environmental factors, (this sport) poses some inherent risk. The authors and publisher advise readers to take full responsibility for their safety and know their limits. Before practicing the skills described in this book, be sure that your equipment is well maintained, and do not take risks beyond your level of experience, aptitude, training, and comfort level. (sports, training)

Dedicated to my father

Joginder Gill

Acknowledgement

Want to thank so many people who made this book happen.

My mother, who has been my support system

My wife, who lived with my chest fat

My mentor, Aditya Ghosh, who believed in me, when noone else did.

My mentor and friend, Nick Parmar, who stood by me

My Friend, Amit Yadav, who got me in the fitness industry

Each one has a role to play and I would not have been here without them.

INTRODUCTION

We Indians especially all the males are obsessed with six-pack abs. The flat stomach, the washboard abs, in simple words, six-pack abs, have now become the gold standard of fitness. Anyone who has abs, is considered to be fit. But there is a fine line between being fit and healthy. I have come across many boys with great physiques but unfit from within. I have seen men, with great set of abs, developing many lifestyle diseases including high blood pressure.

Being aesthetic has its own set of pitfalls. And there is a price one has to pay to look that way, eventually. I am no different. And this is my story or rather undying quest to get that dream body. It's not a manual but a different perspective on the other side of fitness, which has not been addressed so far in the Indian context. The dark side of fitness! The facet no one has ever shown, what people with amazing physiques go through and what you don't see. Surprisingly there are not many books on this subject, and most of it has been my personal experience and my research of interviewing of over three hundred aesthetic Indian bodybuilders and athletes for my fitness YouTube channel.

SO LET'S GET STARTED

Giving up on clothes you love

I was born in the eighties, the era which some of you may relate to. Internationally, eighties was all about beefy men with insane amount of muscles. But in India, where I was born, Sunny Deol, was the quint essential muscular man of the eighties. Raw, strong, and reasonably muscular, not to forget the hairy chest, which back in the days was a sign of being macho.

Well not so much now, considering most of us have now become metrosexual, or in other words, secured with our feminine side. As a child I was conscious about my body, because I always felt there was something unusual about me. The body, which you are not comfortable in!

I always felt that everyone was looking at me or making fun of my body. I was not delusional; I had a legitimate reason, which was my chest. As early as I can remember, I found myself in a very unusual state, which in today's world is called " Man boobs". That is not the only sad part though !

The other sad part is the fact my parents refused to acknowledge this chest fat, which was giving me sleepless nights. And most importantly compromising my self-image, making me feel so helpless. I remember going to my mother and asking her or rather opening up about my chest fat situation. Being the only child, I felt her answer was meant to calm me down! But it aggravated my behavior. She said, my chest is normal and I don't have to worry about anything.

I could see the look on her face when she said that, that is why this whole situation got awkward and aggravated. My response to her answer was not normal at all. " How can it be normal when my chest looks like breast every time I wear a shirt or a t shirt, which is a little fitted". How can it be normal, when everyone else in my class take me as a girl due to my chest size" I said in an angry tone.

But you know how mothers are. They have this amazing knack to convince their child that they are the best, and this is exactly what she did. Made me believe that there is nothing wrong with me, and I am as normal as any other nine-year-old boy. And this is where the problem started. I kept getting bullied at school, for my chest and made fun of, which I could never share or tell anyone at home. Because my mother refused to even recognize that as a problem in the first place.

So what else I could do. I kept taking all the jokes from everyone for next couple of years. I never wore clothes, which would show my chest abnormality. No! There were no special clothes, which could hide that chest problem, I just started wearing lose clothes. When I say loose, I mean really loose. And even my mother agreed with that thought. Even though, I liked wearing fitted clothes, thanks to the influence of actor Sunny Deol, which I described earlier.

This was the first time I realize, what giving up actually means. Giving up on clothes, which I really wanted to wear.

My loved ones told me that I should wear clothes as per my body type. And fitted clothes are not fit for my body. Can you imagine as an eleven year old not to wear clothes which you love and want to buy, but can't. Not because you cannot afford but because you wont be able to wear due to your abnormal body defect, chest fat. And from that day onwards, my whole life changed!

Every time I bought a new shirt or a t shirt, I had to see how my chest looks in it. It was never about the clothes but about how my chest looked in that particular article. This thought kept getting stronger and stronger every year, the thought that I can never wear clothes, which I really like. I wanted to wear tight and skimpy clothes, like actor Salman Khan, even though I knew they don't look that great.

But living in a phobia, is something I was getting comfortable with, every year. I so badly wanted to learn swimming. But I could not. Because I had to take my shirt off in public, which I was never comfortable with. So I also gave up on swimming. I also dread school trips with boys, fearing they may bully me and poke fun at my chest. While all this was happening, I was being pampered at home with food.

I do relate to the thought of being an emotional eater. And I know why fat people eat even when they don't want to eat. And this emotional eating behavior made me fat. So much so that now people officially started calling me fat. As if chest fat was not enough, now I had to live with being fat. Even the lose clothes became tighter and the people who earlier made fun of my chest only now started making fun my whole body. I really didn't know what to do with all this. So I kept skipping school and avoiding meeting people. I became a total recluse, with no friends. My only friend was television, and the cable tv era where they showed one Bollywood movie everyday.

I never went outside to play with the boys, because I was conscious of my fat, I thought it jiggled which it did and made me a laughing stock. So instead I sat at home, ate and watched movies and I must say it was heaven. But it was taking a toll on my health. Literally I was advised by my schoolteacher to see a doctor for my weight issues. But I had given up on all this, because I knew I would still be made fun of. I was so cold, that I didn't even bother telling my parents about it. But my father got a call from my schoolteacher, and was questioned about my sudden weight gain. The teacher was only asking him if I was fine not struggling with any medical illness.

This meeting made my father a totally new person when it came to my health. Within days, he asked me to pick up a sport, which I would like to take up. Very seldom you get such options from your parents, and therefore I picked up something as random as squash. A sport which is played in the four walls amongst two people while the spectators trying to figure out what in hell are they trying to do. And this is where I started playing squash, which changed my life.

CHAPTER 2

The squash days

Playing a sport to get rid of extra flab is probably one of the most tried and tested formula, across the world. But not so effective when it comes to losing chest fat! We will talk about the details of chest fat, what is it and how is it developed in the next few chapters.

My incentive to play squash was very different than my parents. When I picked up squash as a sport it was primarily because I would get a brand new racquet, a kit bag and the shoes which i believe every thirteen year old kid craves. So all it took was one phone call from school to my father on my weight gain and here I was in the squash court exactly after a week with a brand new racquet.

I never knew playing a sport was this difficult, especially when you are overweight. My father had his agenda to make me run so much that I end up losing all the weight in next few weeks. After all squash is considered to be one of the most rigorous sports which can really take a toll on our bodies. I will be honest, the first one year, I had no clue what to do with the racquet, the squash ball was also very tiny with two yellow dots implying the speed of the ball.

The first year was my learning curve, I didn't lose any weight but I definitely picked up the sport, and surprisingly I started loving it. By the time I was fifteen, I was playing reasonably good squash at the club level. But there was a problem! I was not losing weight!

So my father hired a coach for me, who not only taught me basics of the sport but also how to sprint in the court to retrieve the ball. I remember it was 48 year old Dr Bharat Inder Singh, who was extremely ripped and ex paratrooper with a body of a twenty year old. For the first time I saw someone with a six packs.

He was so comfortable with his body that he would change his sweaty clothes right before anyone with ease and people would only look at him in awe. He became my idol. And I only cared about one thing. No matter what, I had to have a body like him. So I asked him, what I could do minimise my body fat, and he coming from the army background, advised me to do running and only running till I get super fit not just for the sport but also for myself.

I started running.

Here is the problem with running, which I felt. First it is boring and second it makes your body lose (when you have chest fat). This has been purely my experience. Even though I was losing weight with running, but I could also see my skin getting lose from the stomach and the chest. On the contrary it made my chest even more lose, what it already was. So one fine day I discussed the problem with Dr. BI Singh about my chest fat.

And he mentioned that it is excessive amount of fat, which will go once I grow up and hit puberty. As per him, it is the influx of testosterone which every young boy goes thru after he turns thirteen and the excessive amount of testosterone can sometimes convert into to estrogen, which is a female hormone. This conversion is usually because of the lifestyle we follow. Considering I was watching movies and eating junk, when I was thirteen, I only made my chest fat situation worse.

But he also assured me that it is fixable if I train hard enough. If I let go of it, it may become a problem for life. That is what happens to most of the kids, I see. They first ignore this problem of chest fat or their parents' inability to understand this problem of chest fat. And once it goes out of whack, it is too late.

So the best way to fix it is around fifteen to eighteen years. Why unnecessarily wait for years only to make it worse. Which is what happened with me. Even though I started losing weight, to an extent I even started looking leaner. But my chest remained as it is.

On the contrary, it started protruding even more. Plus it was lose. So the sport did not help me with chest fat, it only helped me lose weight. This is the misconception of almost everyone in India. Play a sport, and the fat will go, sure it does. But not chest fat. For chest fat, there has to be a different approach.

So my squash career was going really well! Squash even helped me get into India's best college, St Stephens College, Delhi. But the problem remained as it is. I still could not wear the clothes I wanted to, I still had to hide my chest and still my chest would jiggle if I run or play any sport. Because it was lose. I was eighteen, and the problem had become worse. But the good part was, I was looking leaner so I could wear certain clothes, giving people the illusion that I am fit.

Sorry! Can't take off my shirt

But deep down I knew I was not. And when you are in college, you want to be popular for all the right reasons! Luckily my squash was helping me get popular and around that time I got my first girl friend. Everything was perfect! I was in love with her. You know how first love is. But there was this one problem.

She had the best figure and had seen me in my squash clothes, which made me look super fit, and now wanted to see me shirtless. You exactly know where I am going with this. It was time, where we both had to get to the next level of our relationship. But I was never comfortable with my body. I started thinking what would she think if she sees my weird chest fat, she may break up with me or tell her friends about it.

So I started avoiding the question of "why don't you come to my house and hang out ". Where my answer used to be "I had to practice for the upcoming squash tournaments and championships". But for how long I could have avoided this situation. Eventually I had to give in, after all I am a man, who has desires, and as nineteen years old, my sex drive and testosterone was off the roof.

So we finally did it. Luckily she never mentioned the chest part, which made me very happy and thought I may end up marrying her. It feels great when a beautiful girl accepts you for who you are. I mean that's what I thought back then. We kept getting comfortable with each other and then she said what i was afraid of

– Tarun, why is your chest so big and loose.

O man I had no answer to that. She even recommended me that I should start training with weights and hit the gym. You know when the girl you love the most tells you to hit the gym and fix your chest fat, it may hit you a like thunderstorm. You feel ashamed of yourself, and the body you have. So I took her advise not because she was right but because I wanted to look super muscular and prove it to her that I can have the best body as well. And this is where I started my gym to fix the chest fat.

CHAPTER 3

Gym will stop your height ? Really...

I remember being twelve years old and inspired by Sunny Deol's Ghayal, a movie, which not just defined his career but also shaped my future too. After seeing the movie, i was requesting my father to help me get gym membership. But gym back in the days was meant only for bodybuilders, people who want to get beefy and muscular. Surprisingly even after two decades, nothing much has changed in the fitness industry.

Most of the people still consider gym for bodybuilding and pehalwans (Indian terms for bodybuilders and wrestlers) only. And my father always told me like any other parent would, gym will stop your height and growth. This is one of the biggest myths I grew up with and I see many kids in today's generation also get to hear the same thing from their own respective parents.

No one told me that gym can actually minimize my chest fat, and can help me with my sport as well. Had i started gymming when i was thirteen years old, may be my chest fat would have minimized. But as i said, we lacked information and education in the fitness industry, which surprisingly is still the story. Kids are not allowed to train in the gym.

Fitness in India is still considered to be bodybuilding. Fitness is still considered to be big bulging muscles. And people think, that joining a gym guarantees muscles and growth. If that's the case, why do only 1 percent people who are gym goers get to have muscles while remaining ninety percent struggle to put on any muscles.

Anyways, more of that in the following chapters! But here I was, nineteen years old being asked by girl friend that I truly loved to join a gym so I could tighten my chest and look confident. Even though my ego was rubbed but at the same time i was super excited to hit the gym for the first time.

I always wanted to train with weights, because like everyone else in India, I also thought, going to a gym guarantees muscles and body tightness. Super charged up, I entered the gym!

No! Sweating doesn't make you lose fat

Back in the days, there were no air-conditioned gyms only basement gyms where even the fans were not allowed. Why? Because gym trainers and fitness experts of that era thought, that the more you sweat, the more effective your training is. So they would turn off the fans and you would be sweating like a pig, almost experiencing dehydration which the trainers will consider, reward for your hard training.

With that as a backdrop, i entered the gym. Please note, the fitness industry back in the days was not educated enough, still India lacks the fitness infrastructure but back in late nineties, it was all about trainer's experience with weights backed by his tried and tested bodybuilding competition techniques.

So as soon i entered, my weight was checked and was told that i am over weight! What a discovery, as if I didn't know that!

Let me give you personal training

The trainer even made me take my shirt off, which was fine by me, considering this trainer would be the guy who would help me shape my body. But I had no clue what's in store for me. The trainer took notice of my desperation, desperation to minimize my chest fat and offered personal training to me. I didn't know what personal training (PT) was. So without knowing i said yes to personal training and we started weight training.

The trainer told me the cost of personal training, and assured the chest fat will be reduced, a false promise which sometimes most fitness trainers make to get new clients. With that promise, I paid him for personal training after assuring my father, that my chest fat will be reduced and I will be able to perform better in my sport.

Weight training doesn't make you stiff

The first day of training was all about getting accustomed to the weights, which I loved by the way. Anything, which is new, tends to be exciting and I loved every day of weight training. Another myth i was told by my elders that weight training will make you stiff, so whatever you do, lift very light weights. But light weights with no overload will not do anything to the body, on the contrary its a total waste, but hey that's the myth people still follow, and back then I was no different.

I trained with lightweights but after a month of training, I could not see any changes in my body, which my trainer assured. I asked him, why there are no changes, and he in his diplomatic tone, told that it takes 8-16 weeks to see considerable changes in the body. But surprisingly the same trainer said the results start showing in the first week itself, may be I heard it wrong or he was just trying to lure me into personal training.

Take whey proteins damn it

Who knows! Second month into training, the results were still not visible; the trainer recommended I should start looking at supplementing my diet. I didn't understand what he meant. He said I should start taking whey protein. Can you imagine, being told to take whey protein in late nineties what that could mean. I asked my father, about whey protein, obviously he didn't know much about it, and there was no Internet, so he immediately tagged whey protein as steroid.

A powder based substance used for performance enhancement. He even warmed me to stay away from the trainer who was offering me that powder. So here goes my training and my dream to get the body I wanted. Indians usually don't understand the role of supplements in our diet that is why supplements have had a bad reputation in the fitness industry. But luckily things have changed now, thanks to the Internet. But people still think of supplements as a miracle product, which it is not. Even I thought of whey protein as a miracle product, which I thought would change my body, so i had to try.

CHAPTER 4

Whey protein

I was heartbroken, when my father asked me leave weight training on telling him about the supplement which the trainer recommended. Because deep down I thought, whey protein could be the solution to all my chest fat problems. But I really didn't know much about it. And to be honest I didn't even care. All I cared about was that it would give me the body I wanted.

And this is what I see in today's generation as well. They are willing to go to any extreme to get the body of their dreams. I can relate to the desperation, that is why I am sharing this experience so you could learn from my mistakes. This desperation makes them try out dangerous products which can harm their body, and put their life at risk. Even I have done that, more on that in the following chapter.

Coming back to whey protein, my task was to get my hands on whey protein and try it out so I could minimize my chest fat. This would change my body overnight, that's how the trainer described the product to me. This is what I realized; most of the trainers end up doing. Some of them play with people's desperation and take undue advantage of it. Like this trainer, he knew how badly I wanted to change my body especially chest fat, so he played along and gave me hope in the name of whey protein.

And only he knew where to get this product. I didn't have access to amazon, where I would go and search whey protein and it would give me multiple options to choose and I would order, basis trainers recommendation, something which happens today very often.

Convincing parents for whey protein

So for next couple of weeks, I kept thinking about whey protein but no luck at all. The cost of whey protein back in those days was Rupees four thousand for two kgs. This was very expensive for anyone to afford. But in my head, the more expensive the product, better the results!

Years went by and I could not get my hands on whey protein. My college also finished and my body went from bad to worse. And then one day, my father's family friend came whose son in law was a fitness trainer. In India, fitness is still not a mainstream career option and back in those days fitness as a career was restricted to bodybuilding. And bodybuilders in India were considered to be too focused on themselves, I am mildly putting it though, but you know what I mean.

Are bodybuilders dumb ? Don't think so

It is sad, that people think bodybuilders are dumb and can only lift weights. I respect the fact that they put their body through so much stress, but I guess they need to position themselves to come out of this mindset and change people perception. But my father's friend was hell bent on his son-in law to change his profession and get into something, which is more respectable.

Again, it was his perception about the fitness industry. He didn't like the idea, of his son in law training people in their houses or gym and selling box of supplements. Again to each is own.

He wanted my father to speak to his son in law and convince him to change his profession. My father was a very persuasive lawyer and not many people could say no to him. My father agreed and uncle's son in law came to our house. I never knew, his visit to our house would eventually change my life. My father spoke with him on various career options and how open he was to them.

Me on the other hand wanted to speak with him on my chest fat, and how I could fix it. So finally I spoke with him and he also asked me do the same thing, which every trainer did.

Made me take my shirt off. As conscious I was, he made me feel comfortable with my body and told me he could fix this issue of mine. He agreed to train me in his gym where he was working. My father also agreed because he was known to our family and knew he would do the right thing.

Fat burners to minimize chest fat

Once I started training with him, I asked him gently about whey protein, and he immediately refused stating I don't need it at this time. Just when I thought he was credible, he recommended a fat burner, which had ephedra in it. This burner will help me get rid of that extra layer of fat, is what he said. I never told this to my father, but my mother!

And you know how mothers are! They are easy to convince. She agreed. But what surprised me was the cost of that fat burner. That burner costed me Rupees, three thousand that too, only 25 tablets. But I bought it, hoping it will help me with my body. Which it did? I did lose some weight but not so much on my chest.

But the trainer, the family friend, started asking me for money every month for that burner, which I later found out was only for Rupees one thousand with fifty capsules. I was being ripped off and felt cheated but i could not tell my mother about it, because that could have ruined our relations with the family friends. I carried on with it.

Trainer recommending anabolics to fix chest fat

And then after few days, the trainer started recommending me an injectable, which he has used for his bodybuilding competitions. I was so shocked, not because he was recommending me steroids, but because i was known to him. He even assured me nothing will happen, he has used so many times, and I should use it too. He even said, the chest fat wont go if I don't use.

So finally I asked him about the price. I knew he would escalate the price. So instead, I asked him about the product and told him I will ask my friend to get it for me. He refused to even tell me the product/salt name.

No label on products

He said it's a trade secret, which he cannot share! He will only get it and inject for Rupees two thousand per shot. And as per him I would need twenty four shots. Can you imagine someone you know is telling you to use steroids, which he would inject without telling you the name of the drug/ salt.

This was scary and I left everything. And started training on my own with the help of the same fat burner, which he had given. Again years went by but chest fat remained as it is. I even went to the US, to study and could not find a fix to my problem despite trying out various supplements in the market including whey protein.

And then one day, I had a gym friend in the US who recommended me something, which I could never forget. He asked me if I have taken deca durabolin, an anabolic drug, which have been transforming people across the world. And what followed is my experience.

CHAPTER 5

Experience with anabolics

My chest fat made me try out so many things from different health products to food supplements, but nothing technically worked which made me feel comfortable with my body. The thought that I have to live with chest fat for the rest of my life gave me jitters.

But I didn't know what to do. And that gym friend from the US when he recommended Deca Durabolin (DD) it got me thinking. Here in the US i was living by myself, which means I could try anything I could without anyone's approval.

Also I was self sufficient making money from doing small time jobs, so I could afford this drug too. Now all I had to do was research a bit on what DD is all about. Thankfully, the Internet was at its full swing and I gathered as much information as I could.

When it comes to choosing anabolic, the first thing you look up are the side effects, and DD had the least of sides, which gave me comfort. And then finally I took the plunge and experimented with anabolics with the condition that the guy who recommended DD will now have to administer and inject the shot as well. He happily agreed.

My first needle experience

I remember the first shot I took of DD, gave me headache, and high fever. For which I was prepared, since the gym friend has forewarned me about the initial side effects, which would eventually subside. The recommended dosage which was mentioned on the website when I researched was 300 mgs/week for a beginner. So I went with that.

Its funny, that even today, google search is dictating everyone first steroid cycle. Which to me can be very dangerous, you will see shortly. Now the moment you start injecting, you start feeling like a superman, even though it is psychological. My main reason to inject was to get rid of chest fat. But to my surprise, DD made my chest fat even worse.

Wrong steroid will make the condition worse

Because no one told me that DD gives you water retention and makes you fat because it increases your appetite. I kept eating and my chest fat kept getting worse. I thought this is muscle, which I am putting on, but I was wrong. My chest fat had gone worse and now it started looking like breasts. Can you imagine, a boy in a foreign land injecting drugs to make his body worse with no guidance or supervision or medical monitoring.

This was my case. I took couple of shots and eventually gave up seeing my chest condition. I simply chose the wrong drug, and this is what happens in India too. When kids who may be struggling with the same problem, are being told to inject either Test or DD.

Masturbation

When I stopped taking DD, someone told me about impotency using DD. And it gets worse if it is taken standalone without using any testosterone as a base. And that was me! So I started masturbating more, just to see if I am impotent, which I was not. Thank God.

Feeling blessed, I decided not to ever touch anabolics in life ever again. So I came back after finishing my MBA and started my corporate career. Even though I was working, my mind always found reasons to train and hit the gym. I kept training alongside by taking only whey protein post work out. I did that for about couple of years gradually giving up on my dream of having a best body.

Even though I was helpless to fix my chest fat, I started reading about fitness, enrolled myself for online fitness certifications, which changed my life. The certifications gave me a whole new dimension to training and how to fix chest fat. The following chapters are about how I fixed my chest fat and transformed myself

PART 2

Fixing chest fat

Can you fix chest fat

Before addressing the issue on how I fixed my chest fat, it is important to understand what is chest fat. Now chest fat is common problem amongst many men, which usually starts at an early age of eleven years.

This could be due to their sedentary lifestyle or it may very well be running in their family. My father had chest fat, which was not too prevalent but I had a worse one because I didn't have an active lifestyle while growing up.

Chest fat, which is also called "Man boobs" these days, is nothing but an enlargement of breast tissue in men caused by fat built around nipples. If aggravated, these man boobs can turn into gynecomastia, which is growth of excessive breast tissue in men.

I wish back in the days someone had told me this definition, but unfortunately I had no visibility to such conditions prevalent amongst men. And now these conditions are very common.

But the question is "Can you fix chest fat" Here is a simple answer to this question

Chest fat can be minimized but if the condition has worsened or has turned into Gynecomastia, commonly referred to as Gyno, then the only cure is a surgery. But I feel even Gynecomastia can be cured to about eighty percent.

I fixed my chest fat that everyone thought was gyno, but now i am super comfortable with my body type and happy to share what exactly I did to fix it.

HOW I FIXED MY CHEST FAT

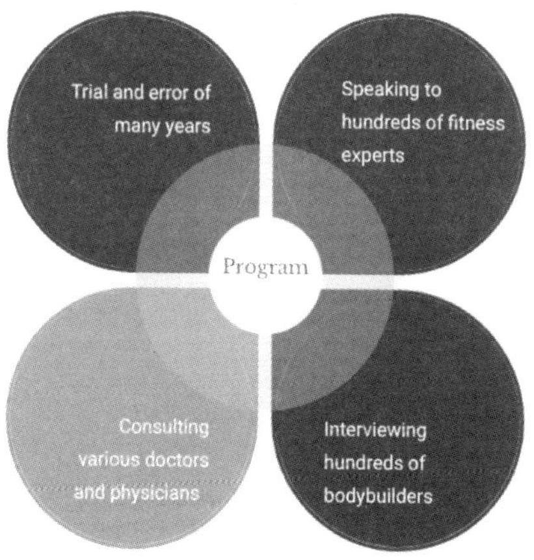

Please note this book is an amalgamation of

- Trial and error of many years
- Speaking to hundreds of fitness experts
- Interviewing hundreds of bodybuilders for my fitness YouTube channel
- Consulting various doctors and physicians

The tripod to minimize chest fat

Now that you know that you can minimize chest fat, you need to prepare your action plan. This action plan will revolve around three things. It doesn't matter what your body type is or what's your age, color and nationality, you just need to treat these three things as your fitness tripod for next 12 weeks, lets call it 90 days.

How long will it take for this plan to work?

The answer is simple again, give yourself 90 days to transform not just your chest fat but also your physical and mental well being. Because once you take charge of your mental well being, the physical goal will become extremely easy and clear.

Your fitness tripod viz Mind, Training and Food. These are the only three things, which we will be working on this 90 days journey.

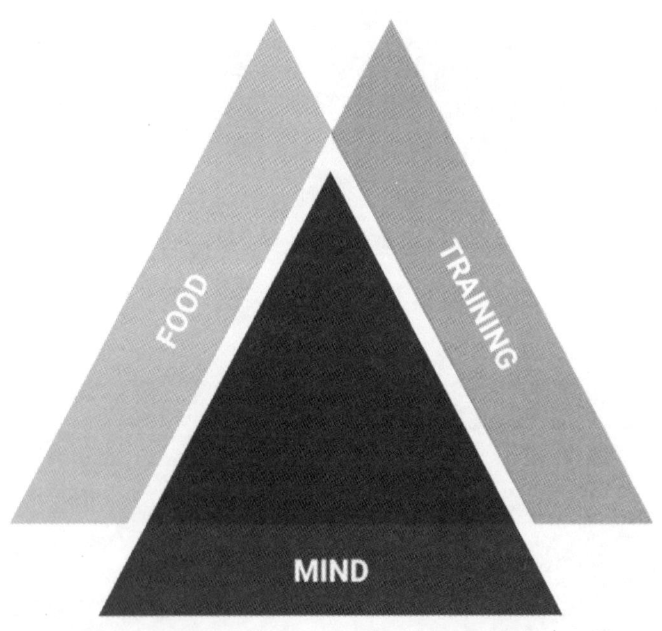

1 MIND

I must have read at least five hundred fitness books on how to get rid of chest fat, spoke to thousands of fitness trainers and to my surprise none of them mentioned the role of our mind, in transforming our body. All they talked about was diet and training programs. But let me tell you something, training programs wont work, the diet won't work unless you mind is convinced that you can achieve the body you want.

Unless you convince your mind that you will flatten your chest fat! Everything starts with your mind. You have to visualize how you want to look like. All these years, I knew I had a problem of chest fat, but what was missing is how I would look if I were to minimize my chest fat.

The picture was missing, because I never visualized the picture of how I would look like when I meet my fitness goal. And because of which, my mind was not convinced and never promoted me to take concrete action. Because I never fed my mind, with the conviction that I can do it. This is what the problem is with everyone.

We don't have a goal.

We have a problem, which we tell everyone. I am fat, I have chest fat, and the same problem we are feeding our mind as well. Instead we should be telling ourselves every frigging day that I can and I will achieve the body I want.

It's called the Law of attraction. If you put it out there in the universe, the whole universe will try to help you with your dream body. But we just don't. Instead we keep feeding our mind with all the negativity of what we have been through with the body we have. And how our life has become a living hell. Trust me, all these years this is exactly what I was doing too.

Now here is what you would do

Visualize

Give yourself a goal. Put a picture of whom you want to look like. It could be any actor or a person who you look up to. But give your mind something to visualize. Only when you visualize, the mind will start working. I am sure you saw Pumping Iron, where the legendary Arnold, talked about the importance of visualization. (If you have not seen it, it is available on NetFlix)

This tool of visualization became one of his success mantra, which he proudly shares with the world. He first visualized, he wanted to become Mr Olympia by having the best physique in the business. He first visualized that he would become Hollywood's most desirable and successful actor. And later he first visualized he would get into politics and eventually become a Mayor of US most powerful state.

If you don't visualize in your mind, you are not getting anywhere. Let me tell you something, you can have the best trainer on board and have the best nutritionist to help you with your fitness goal, you will not get anywhere close to your goal, unless you have visualized your goal.

We are stuck

The problem with most of us that we are stuck with training programs! What training program can we follow to get to our goal. That is why fitness companies offer life changing training programs for a heavy price, knowing people will buy.

Because the pop culture has made us believe that fitness has everything to do with the training program one follow. The more expensive the program, better the results, is what we are made to believe. Remember I shared previously I had the same problem the more expensive the product, better the result!

Programs come much later, but just imagine, if you are weak, not strong enough to change your body, for how long can you follow the program. You will eventually get bored and start looking for different programs. That is what happens to most of us. How often do we change our training programs, I am sure very often. Not because the training program is ineffective but our mind is not strong enough to follow thru with the program.

It doesn't matter what training program you follow, it is science, when you train with weights, your body will respond. But how you are connecting your mind to the muscle is where the game lies. Now that brings me to a new topic of visualization–mind to muscle.

Mind to muscle connection

Do you know 90% of the people who go to the gym train only physically? What I mean is that they only show their face to the gym but when it comes to training, their mind is all over the place. Cross your heart and tell me that you don't do that yourself.

I was making that mistake for years where I would just go to the gym and tell the world, I trained for two hours or ran for 10 kms on a treadmill. These days we do that for our social media presence. Before we even step a foot in a gym, our status is already updated on our social handles. So technically we are only training for people who we are desperately trying to impress. If this is your approach to training, let me tell you, might as well give up on your dream to have the best body. Unless and until you connect your mind to the working muscle you are training, you will not get any results. This is what you need to change

Spend 5 minutes with yourself

When you enter your gym, turn off your phone and any communication device, which distracts you from your fitness routine. Remember you are in the gym to come one step closer to your fitness goal. By distracting yourself and talking to others you are only delaying the process.

Before you start your training program, it is important for you to talk to yourself for five minutes. Spend time alone and prep your work out on what you plan to do. What I was doing was the opposite. After entering the gym, I would decide what body part do I really need to train. If I see my friend training chest, I would go start training chest. Remember it is about your goal, work as per that, not as per your friend's convenience.

Your goal should be everywhere

Put a picture of how you want to look like on your phone. It is ok to have your girl friend or wife on your phone cover. But not for another 90 days.

You need to constantly bombard your mind with the picture of how you would look like in next 90 days. Remember you are feeding your mind with a picture or a visual, which only the mind has created. Make it work 24 by 7.

No negative thoughts.

There will be times when you would want to give up and feel that the goal is impossible to achieve. Remember only you can fix that negativity then and there. Don't nurture that thought. Immediately start seeing motivational videos of people who have done the impossible. Or start watching pictures and videos of people who inspire you.

If you let these negative thoughts take charge, you will ruin your work out because you have lost the motivation. Keep your mind focused on the positives. I know it is tough but you are in control of your thoughts, not the other way round.

Read Read and read some more

It is important for you to keep your mind focused on the right things.

Remember transformation is not just physical but also mental. By the end of 90 days, you would not only be strong mentally, but also physically.

Read books, the ones I recommend are-

- Believe in Yourself by Dr Joseph Murphy
- Miracles of your mind by Dr Joseph Murphy
- Catalyst by ChandraMouli Venkatasan
- The power of Habit by Charles Duhigg
- Inner Engineering by Sadhguru

These books will keep you positive and consistently feed you with the arsenal you need for your brain.

2 Training

We talked about mental training in the last section, now we talk about the physical training specifically for chest. All these years i kept wondering if there is any specific exercise to reduce chest fat.

Yes there are certain exercises you need to do everyday.

YOU HEARD ME RIGHT- EVERYDAY

Please note, we people who are struggling with chest fat cannot rely on a traditional training program of Back, Biceps, Chest triceps legs shoulders etc.

We need to hit chest everyday to ensure it is in shape. It requires lot of effort but there is no escape from this.

So lets get started.

Chest training

I followed a conventional training program for years, which included, same old techniques, Arnold preached back in seventies. I am not saying that doesn't work but lets face it. Arnold was not struggling with chest fat.

So we cannot follow his training methodology. Though we will include certain exercises, which can come in handy.

Weaker area first

For you to minimize your chest fat in 90 days, you need to be super focused on your chest more than any other body part. Because this is the pain area, which needs immediate attention! My problem was that I loved training shoulders. As a result, my shoulders kept getting stronger, making my chest looks even more weaker and saggy.

On the contrary I should have trained my shoulders less. But that's normal. I am sure you also have a favorite body part, which you love to train. But please don't focus on your favorite body part, focus on your pain areas first.

Engage chest everyday

Whatever you do, you have to train and engage your chest everyday. Now the conventional wisdom says, if we were to train one body part everyday how are we going to grow that body train because we are not giving enough time to recover. Which is true in most cases, but we don't want to grow our chest, we only want to attack our chest fat so we break the fat cells from it. The growth of chest muscle comes much later.

The chest exercise you must do everyday

One old school exercise, which you can never ignore and is my best friend and will become your best friend, too is a classic Push up.

Remember we need to do push ups to ensure our chest remains tight. What usually happens is that we often train our chest twice a week, with the same set of exercises, which doesn't allow the chest fat cells to break often resulting in stagnation.

The best way to incorporate push ups in your daily training routine is in a warm up. Do at least 4-6 sets of 25 repetitions. You must do 100 push ups everyday, without fail.

Remember the idea is to prepare your chest for the excessive load via training. And push up will do just that. Don't tell me that you cant do push ups! Well if you cant, you should not even be training in the first place. Stop reading this manual if you cant do push ups.

Running is a big NO NO

Now if you have read the first section of the book, i was told by my coaches to run and do cardio if I wanted to get minimize chest fat. But little did I know, running was only making it worse.

I noticed, every time I did a cardio session, my chest became lose and saggy, whereas a good push up session made it tighter.

So it became very evident for me, that I would choose push-ups over running any day. I am not saying don't do cardio at all. Remember cardio is good for your heart, you must add a session or two every week, but not running. You may choose to do cycling, or stairmaster.

One big secret about cardio

If you are struggling with chest fat, one secret, which no one shares with the world is when should they be doing the cardio. Before weight training or after weight training.

So here is the answer-

CARDIO- Always do it after your weight training.

For person who is trying to minimize chest fat, it is always recommended that they do cardio that too stairmaster or cycling after their weight training. Remember your focus is to minimize chest fat not become a marathon runner by running for hours. Since we are talking about marathon, look at all the marathon runners! They have high body fat and reasonably lose skin compare to sprinters who focuses more on strength training. This should give you some perspective.

Training schedule–how often should you train

This is the question I was struggling for years! How much is too much and how less is too less. So what I figured and recommend to people with chest fat is to train minimum five days a week. Anything less than 5 days is too less.

Training focus out of those five days has to be chest- which means three dedicated work outs every week for chest.

Here is a sample program, which will give you an idea. But keep changing exercises as per your level.

MONDAY

TARGET AREA: CHEST AND ARMS

Warm up- Push ups, 100

Remember, We don't change this work out, this will be our standard chest work out for next 90 days. I know it can be boring, but believe me you will thank me for it.

Photo Credits - Weight Training Guide

MAIN WORKOUT

Exercise # 1: INCLINE BARBELL PRESS- 4 SETS, 15 REPETITIONS

Exercise #2: INCLINE DUMBBELLS PRESS- 4 SETS, 15 REPETITIONS

Photo Credits - Weight Training Guide

EXERCISE #3 DUMBBELL PULLOVER - 4 SETS, 15 REPETITIONS

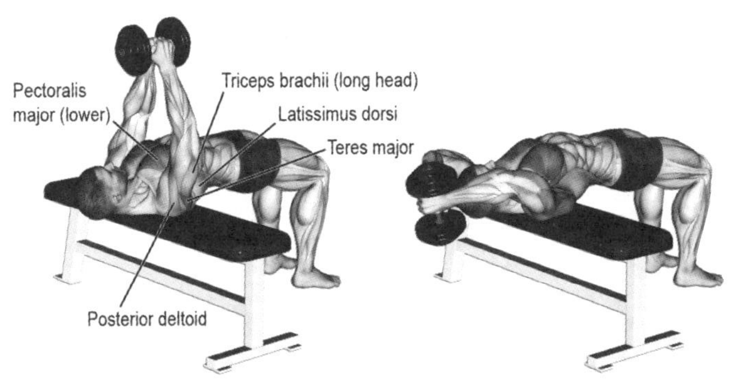

EXERCISE # 4 CABLE CROSS-OVER- 4 SETS, 15 REPETITIONS

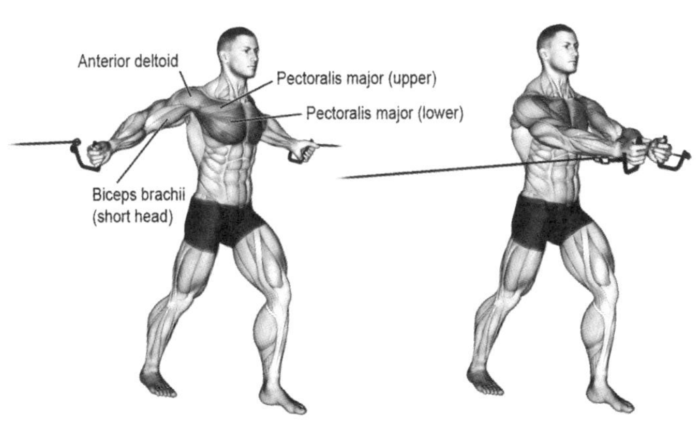

Photo Credits - Weight Training Guide

EXERCISE # 5 FLAT BENCH PRESS- 4 SETS, 15 REPETITIONS

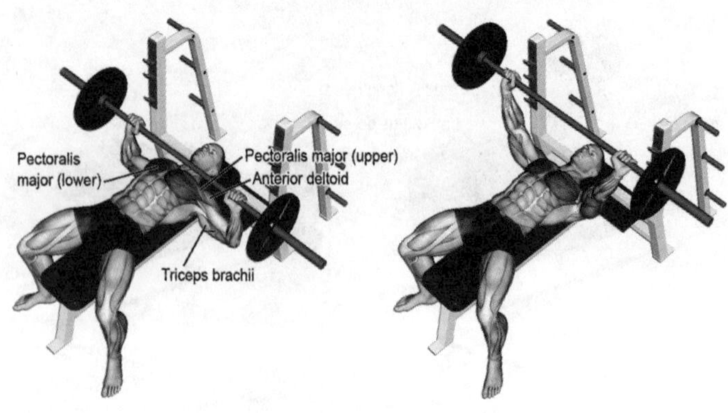

EXERCISE # 6 MACHINE PRESS- 4 SETS, 15 REPETITIONS

Photo Credits - Weight Training Guide

EXERCISE # 7 TRICEPS PUSH DOWN - 4 SETS, 15 REPETITIONS

or

EXERCISE # 7 DUMBBELL TRICEPS EXTENSION - 4 SETS, 15 REPETITIONS

Photo Credits - Weight Training Guide

EXERCISE # 8 BICEPS BARBELL CURLS- 4 SETS, 15 REPETITIONS

EXERCISE # 9 DUMBELL CURLS- 4 SETS, 15 REPETITIONS

Photo Credits - Weight Training Guide

TUESDAY

Exercise # 10 Cycling 30 minutes

TARGET AREA: SHOULDERS AND LEGS

Warm up- Push ups, 100

Photo Credits - Weight Training Guide

MAIN WORKOUT

EXERCISE # 1 DUMBBELL SHOULDER PRESS- 4 SETS, 15 REPETITIONS

EXERCISE # 2 ARNOLD PRESS- 4 SETS, 15 REPETITIONS

Photo Credits - Weight Training Guide

EXERCISE # 3 DUMBBELL SIDE LATERALS- 4 SETS, 15 REPETITIONS

EXERCISE # 4 DUMBBELL FRONT RAISES- 4 SETS, 15 REPETITIONS

Photo Credits - Weight Training Guide

EXERCISE # 5 DUMBBELL SHRUGS - 4 SETS, 15 REPETITIONS

Photo Credits - Weight Training Guide

EXERCISE # 6 FREE SQUATS- 4 SETS, 15 REPETITIONS

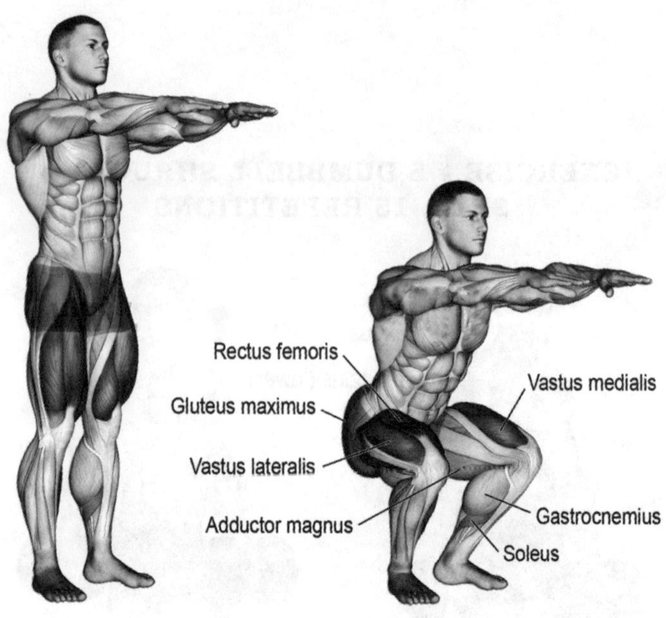

EXERCISE # 7 LEG EXTENSION- 4 SETS, 15 REPETITIONS

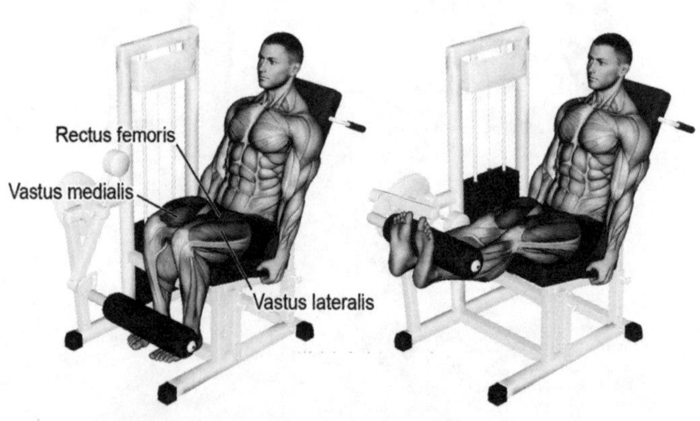

Photo Credits - Weight Training Guide

EXERCISE # 8 DEADLIFT- 4 SETS, 15 REPETITIONS

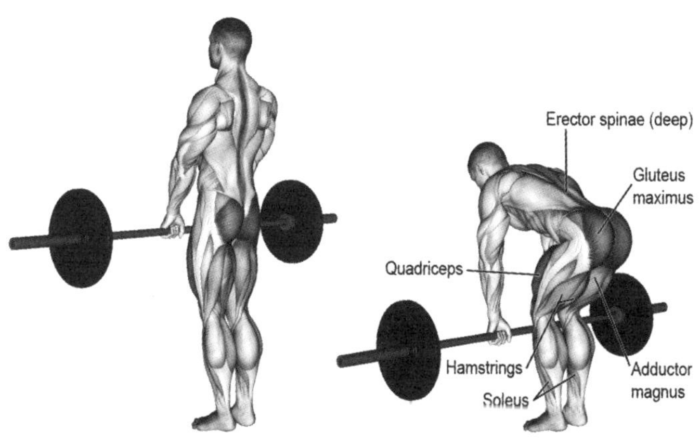

EXERCISE # 9 DUMBBELL CHEST FLY- 4 SETS, 15 REPETITIONS

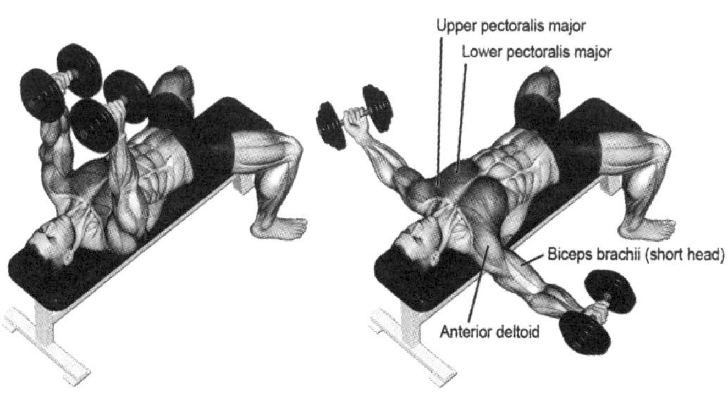

Photo Credits - Weight Training Guide

YES YOU HAVE TO DO CHEST FLIES ON SHOULDER DAY TOO. ☺

WEDNESDAY

REPEAT MONDAY

THURSDAY

TARGET AREA: BACK AND SHOULDERS

Warm Up: Push Ups 100

Photo Credits - Weight Training Guide

MAIN WORKOUT

EXERCISE # 1 LAT PULL DOWN - 4 SETS, 15 REPETITIONS

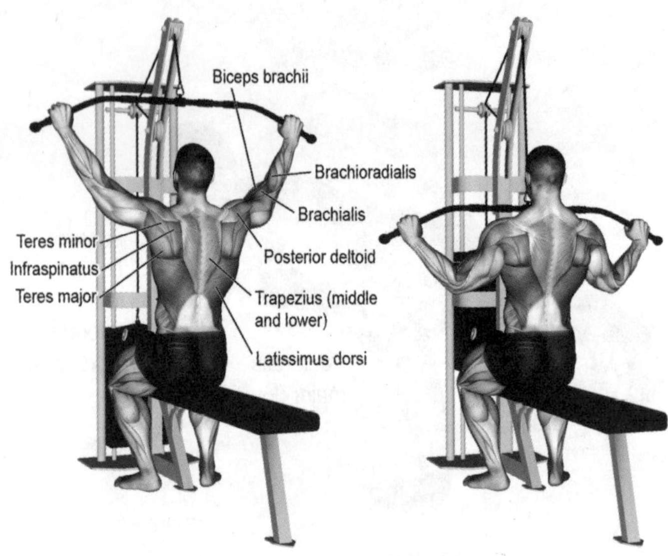

EXERCISE # 2 CLOSE GRIP PULL DOWN- 4 SETS, 15 REPETITIONS

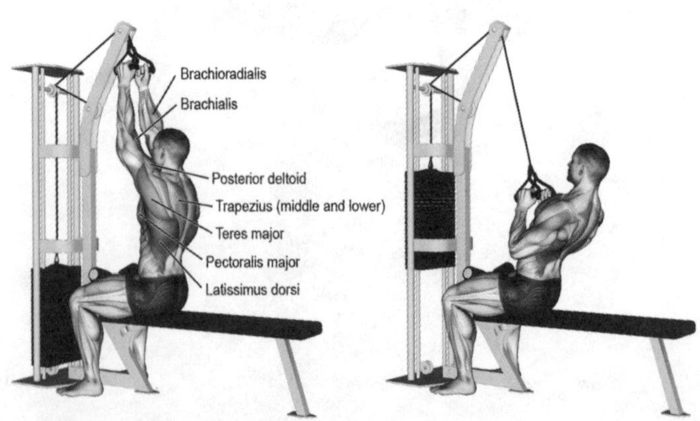

Photo Credits - Weight Training Guide

EXERCISE # 3 PULL UPS- 4 SETS, 15 REPETITIONS

EXERCISE # 4 SINGLE ARM ROWING- 4 SETS, 15 REPETITIONS.

Photo Credits - Weight Training Guide

EXERCISE # 5 DEADLIFTS - 4 SETS, 15 REPETITIONS

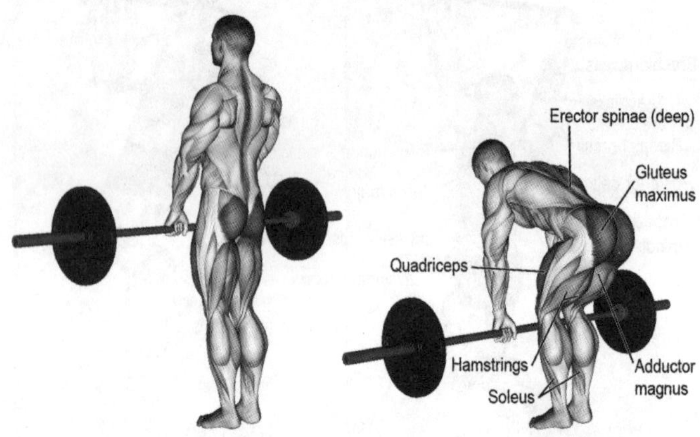

EXERCISE # 6 DUMBBELL SHOULDER PRESS- 4 SETS, 15 REPETITIONS

Photo Credits - Weight Training Guide

EXERCISE # 7 ARNOLD PRESS- 4 SETS, 15 REPETITIONS

Photo Credits - Weight Training Guide

EXERCISE # 8 DUMBBELL SHRUGS - 4 SETS, 15 REPETITIONS

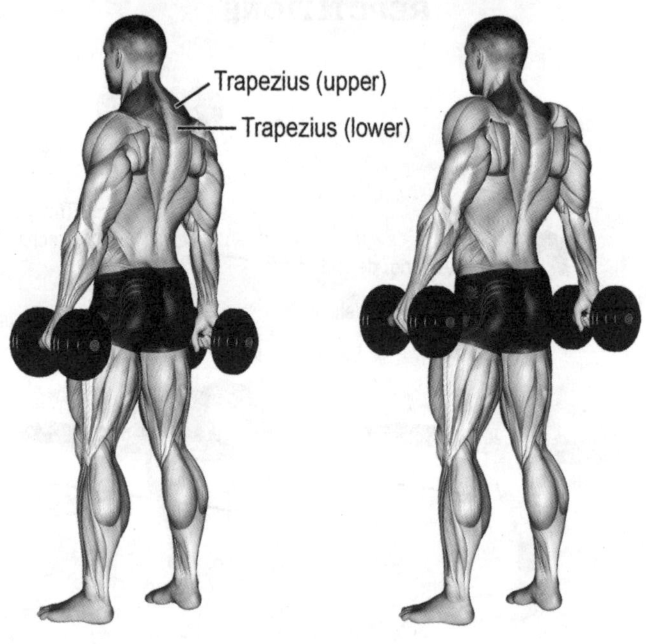

Photo Credits - Weight Training Guide

EXERCISE # 9 INCLINE DUMMBELL FLY- 4 SETS, 15 REPETITIONS

Photo Credits - Weight Training Guide

EXERCISE # 10
CARDIO CYCLING 30 MINUTES

FRIDAY

REST

This is where you recover from your workouts! The diet on this day will follow in my next segment

SATURDAY

Target Area: Chest only

Warm up: Push Ups 100

Photo Credits - Weight Training Guide

EXERCISE # 1 PULL UPS - 100

EXERCISE # 2 DUMBBELL PULL OVER- 4 SETS, 15 REPETITIONS

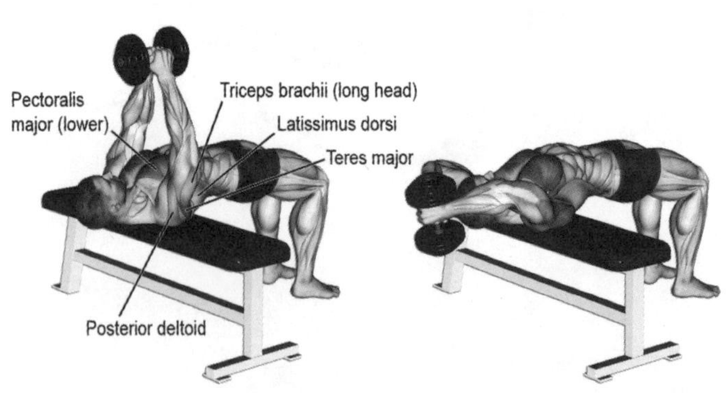

Photo Credits - Weight Training Guide

EXERCISE # 3 CABLE CROSS OVER- 4 SETS, 15 REPETITIONS

EXERCISE # 4 PUSH UPS- 200

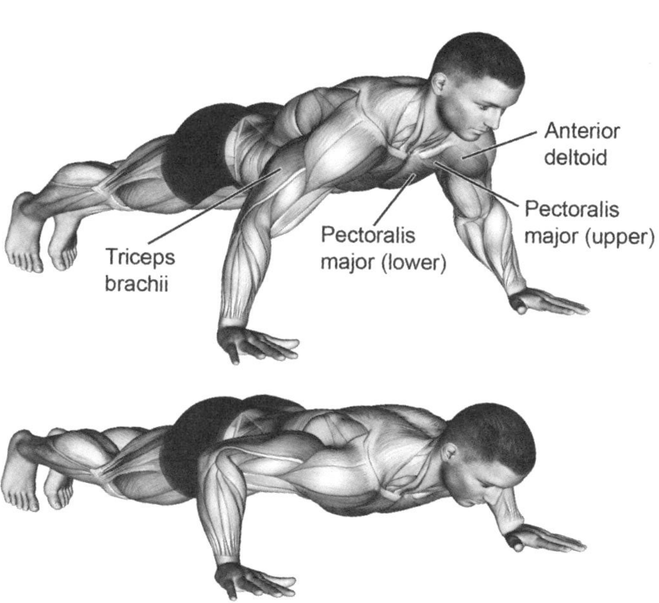

Photo Credits - Weight Training Guide

EXERCISE # 5 FLAT DUMBELL FLY- 4 SETS, 15 REPETITIONS

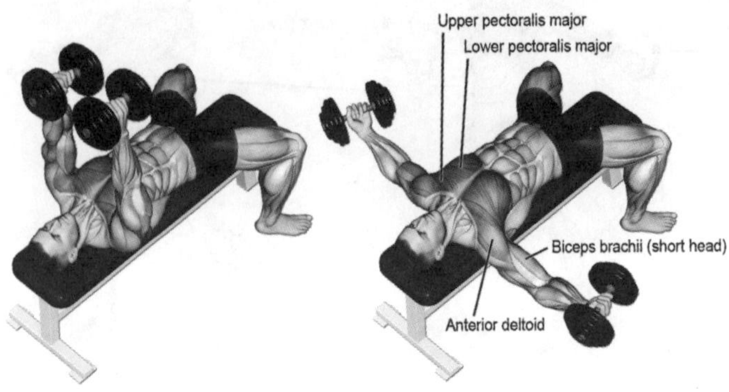

EXERCISE # 6 FLAT BENCH PRESS- 4 SETS, 15 REPETITIONS

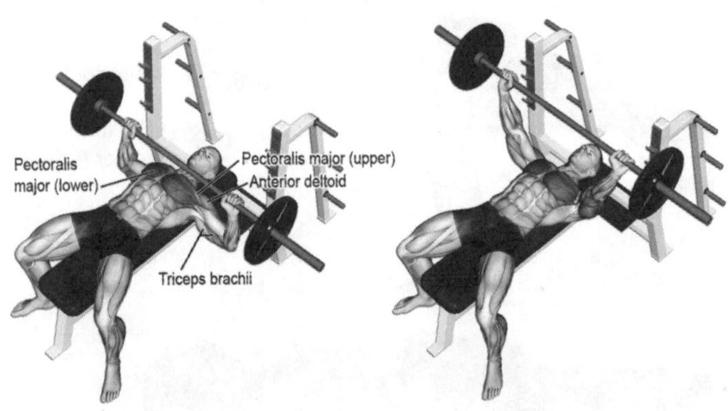

Photo Credits - Weight Training Guide

EXERCISE # 7 INCLINE PRESS- 4 SETS, 15 REPETITIONS

Photo Credits - Weight Training Guide

EXERCISE # 8 INCLINE DUMBBELL FLY- 4 SETS, 15 REPETITIONS

Photo Credits - Weight Training Guide

EXERCISE # 9
CARDIO CYCLING 45 MINUTES

SUNDAY

Only Cardio for 1 hour

DIET/FOOD/NUTRITION

This is the third segment or rather the third pillar of our fitness tripod. Your mind has given you the picture. The training, which you have embarked upon execution of that visualization and food is now the discipline which will keep it together. Before we get into the diet, there are certain things I want you to remember

Discipline

Discipline is the key to successful dieting. The more you practice discipline, the better you get at it. Anytime you feel hungry, just divert your mind from your hunger. It is ok to starve than to put something in your body, which you may regret later.

Cravings

Craving is one of your biggest enemy which will bother you from time to time. This craving can be of sugar or junk. Remember you need to curb this craving.

How to curb your craving ? Simple

See yourself in the mirror and tell yourself. If you eat this, it will put you right where you had started. It will be very challenging in the beginning, but once you start seeing the results, you will be motivated enough to say no to anything.

Cheat meal

There will be a cheat meal for you every week, more of a reward for being a good boy. Wait for that meal, dont just have cheat meals every day. Have explained the concept of cheat meals in the next segment.

THE DIET-KEEPING IT SIMPLE

We need to have food items, which can naturally increase our test levels and lower our estrogen. In other words, stay away from food, which has more sugar and oil in them. Here is your typical diet, which you can manipulate for 90 days.

- **Breakfast- Oats Pre lunch- apple/ orange**

- **Lunch- 150 grams of chicken breast/ Fish and green salad**

- **Veg options- Dal/75 grams paneer/ cottage cheese**

- **Post lunch- Black coffee/Black tea**

- **Evening snack- Peanuts plain/green salad**

- **Dinner- Fish 150 grams/salad**

- **Veg options-Dal/75 grams paneer/ cottage cheese**

Now this is a very boring diet to be followed for next 90 days. But once you start seeing the results, you will start loving this diet. I have been following it for days now and still love it.

Whenever you feel the need for beverage, sip on black coffee.

Carbs in losing chest fat

If you see, the diet is very low carb and there is a reason for that. I have seen it on people and myself that every time there is an increase of carb in the diet, i start gaining water weight. People with chest fat are more prone to gaining fat, and having more carbs in the diet may lead to more fat accumulation in the chest area. This is one of the reasons why we don't need too many carbs in the diet for us to minimize chest fat.

Now many people will feel that how can they survive without the carbs. They need their rice and rotis. But remember carbs are not bad, it's the timing of carbs which is bad and delays the results.

If you really feel the need for carbs, have it before your weight training session that also a sweet potato or oats. Complex carbs is what you should be focused on.

Food to avoid

This section you may not like because I would be telling you to stop or rather minimize the food items you may love. But it is for your own good. It has taken me years to come up with this permutation and combination, on what actually works.

If you are a diary lover and cant sleep without having milk, I suggest you now get used to sleeping without that glass of milk. Milk and some dairy products are a big no no in this program, barring of course some low fat cottage cheese.

Milk Sugar:

I have realized can make things worse for people with chest fat. This I have not only tried on myself but on many others who were struggling to lose their chest fat.

Soya:

This is a plant which contains high estrogen, a female hormone. Now there have been many studies around this. Some say it wont cause male boobs and some would say it would aggravate the situation. Soya despite high and rich in protein did not suit me. And I won't recommend it. You can try it out but as part of this program, I would stay away from it.

Junk/Fried:

Now this is self explanatory. But you should also avoid red meat and canned food. Again that is my experience. When it comes to food, everyone has their own experience. I would recommend what has worked on me.

Alcohol – If you are beer drinker, you may not like this. Alcohol believer it or not, severely affects our liver ability to remove extra estrogens from our body. More estrogen means more chest fat. Remember in simple terms extra estrogen is our enemy. (Trust me this can be a game changer)

Anti estrogen food to add:

Broccoli, Vinegar (Awesome when it comes to metabolizing carbs, this can be your best friend)

Walnuts

Almonds

Avocados

Pomegranates

Spinach

Cauliflower

Eggs

Vinegar

Daily formula multivitamin

Universal Nutrition Animal Whey

All the above food items are anti estrogen which means they will not only naturally help you increase your test levels but also slow down the carb absorption which may lead to fat gain.

Supplements to add

- Whey protein–2 scoops post work out
- Glutamine- 5 grams before going off to sleep
- BCAA- Intra work out
- Fat Burner/Caffeine- Before training
- Arbuterol- Quick water loss formula
- Multi vitamins- one with breakfast
- Fish oil- with breakfast
- Test Grow–Natrual test booster by Universal Nutrition.
- ZMA- this will help you sleep better and minimize your stress levels .

These are the only supplements you need.

Minimize Stress levels

I realized much later that one of the main reasons for my chest fat, was actually stress. Stress hormone cortisol can spell disaster for our physical health. I know it can be hard ot keep the stress levels in check but trust me it is for your own good.

Do you need anabolics

I will be honest with you!

If you were to follow the fitness tripod, you would not need any help from anabolics or steroids. Simply because you are not trying to compete or become a bodybuilder. I have shared in my previous section, I have used it and have experienced side effects too, that is why i will never recommend the use of anabolics in this transformation.

You are not alone, there are so many men who were struggling with chest fat and finally managed to fix it. What did they do.

This section is a collection of short stories, which will motivate you.

There are many guys out there who are struggling with chest fat. But some of them are constantly fighting it out to fix this for good. My platform TG Talks, India's most effective digital platform, allows me to meet many such people.

Via TG Talks I try to capture people's fitness journeys and what they have been through in the form of an interview. These inspiring stories/interviews are consumed within my large social media network of over one million.

TG Talks made me meet many such boys who were struggling with the issue of chest fat. So much so that some even tried to commit suicide with the self-image they saw of themselves in the mirror.

I want to share some stories, which will tell you how much of a problem chest fat has become amongst men of all ages.

I tried to wear my mother's bra.

Very recently I met up with this twenty-year-old good-looking guy "Vyomesh" who approached me for an interview on TG Talks. His friend messaged me on Instagram and shared his physical transformation. But I believe physical transformation is a lot easier than a mind or we call it a mental transformation. Unless you are mentally tough, physical transformation will never give you the desired results.

But when she shared his mental transformation of abuse and bullying what he had gone through in school, it made me feel that this story should be told to the larger audience. So, I called him to the show and he shared some incidents, which shook me to the core.

As a kid, our parents try their best to give us all that they can to pamper our childhood. I have also seen some parents who are absolutely ok with their kids putting on extra weight which they feel is baby fat and will go as they turn into an adult. But that seldom happens. This exactly happened with Vyom.

His mother made him eat a lot. You know how mothers are, they always feel that their kid is undernourished. His mother kept showing him with her love in the form of good food and Vyom kept eating and eating.

Within months Vyom started feeling heavy so much so that he could barely carry his own weight. Some kids started pointing out in school but when he came back home, his mother always made him feel secured and assured him there is nothing wrong with him. Which gave him confidence that he is not fat.

Ideally his mother should have paid attention and could have minimise his daily calorie intake but as I said mothers are so loving that they forget that their love sometimes can become their child's worst nightmare.

Vyom kept eating for months, and his mother kept protecting him. Vyom also should have made an effort to stop this eating spree, but as you put on more and more weight, food becomes an emotional need not a physical one.

He was a very confident young kid. But as the fat kept gaining prominence in his body, his confidence level began to shatter. His school mates kept poking fun at his fat body especially his chest area. A point came he even stopped telling his mother what he was going through in school. Because deep down he now knew she would always try to be a mother and would be biased.

The situation became so worse that even his relatives started to notice his weight gain and made fun of him. He now had nowhere to go. He was anyways a subject of joke in school and now even at home, he was being considered abnormal, a fat kid.

It just didn't end there. The fun had now taken a form of bullying and abusing. Bullies don't just attack your body but also your self image. They not only harm you physically but also kill your inner belief. Taunts can still be bearable but when someone tries to attack you in a group that too on your weakness, it hurts.

The bully experience

Vyom shared that horrific incident when a group of young bullies cornered him with a compass in their hands. They were threatening him to puncture his chest fat. They forcibly dragged him into men's washroom and started unbuttoning his shirt.

Surprisingly Vyom did not even retaliate, he felt helpless. He just stood there while those kids kept groping him. All he could do was cry. He recalls that he had so much of fat that even when he walked, his whole body fat jiggled. A site like that always invites a bully. And that's exactly what happened that day.

He could not do anything. He was 130 kgs and five feet five inches. You can imagine how big he would be. Plus with a weight like that, he became an easy prey. Even while people bullied him, he could not even scream out loud for help. He just surrendered

Because I didn't raise my voice, that compass incident of boys ganging up against me in a group kept repeating. Then one day I got so fed up, that I decided not to go to school anymore. I had no courage to face those boys. Whenever I would think of school, the horrific images of those boys popped into my head, which stopped me from attending any classes.

But the bullies didn't stop. Vyom's younger brother was also in the same school. The bullies got hold of him and started doing the same what they were doing to Vyom.

Elder brother is supposed to protect the younger one, but in this case I was such a coward, I could not even protect my little brother from these bullies.

That incident got the worse out of me, recalls Vyom. That episode changed me. I knew I had to do something or this could get really ugly. Why would they attack my brother? He was two years younger to me. His younger brother came back home that day and cried like a baby. This episode in itself was good enough to fuel the fire inside Vyom.

Vyom wanted to be the role model for his younger brother. But hiding from bullies and not doing anything about it is not the example he wanted to set for his brother.

I wanted the real me to come out. The one who is free, confident and don't take anything from anyone. But I could not find that guy inside. The bullies killed him. I wanted to awaken him but that change needed a lot of effort and it wasn't easy, said Vyom.

I was so neck deep into this pile of fat that it was almost impossible for me to come out of it. So I thought why not create an illusion, which would appear that everything in my body is normal. I wasn't ashamed of my belly fat but my chest fat because chest fat looked a lot like boobs. Can you imagine a man who has boobs, what is that feeling!

Male boobs

I wanted to hide my male boobs. So then all kinds of thoughts started coming into my head. While I was in the washroom, I saw my mother's bra and a weird thought came into my head. Why don't I try wearing my mother's bra to tighten up my chest fat? I thought might be this illusion could help me savage this extreme situation of excessive chest fat or rather male boobs.

So I wore the bra and looked at myself in the mirror. That sight made me hate myself. Here I was, a sixteen-year-old boy trying out my mother's bra to hide my chest fat looking directly into the mirror.

This incident triggered a spark. A spark, which made me believe that what the hell am I doing with my life. This is not me. I need to change this.

Even the health was not on my side. Because the excessive weight I was carrying, even my health was deteriorating. My legs had given up on me. This was a stage where I was limping. I used to cry every night to my mother, that what have I done to myself. Please help me. And even she had no answer. She would just listen and put me to sleep.

My parents now had no option but to take me to a doctor for a health check up.

The doctor recommended a fat loss surgery. Because the longer I carry the excessive weight the worse the situation would get on my legs.

I should have been happier that finally I will go under the knife and all the weight will disappear. But something stopped me from going for this surgery. I needed a vision and I suddenly had found the vision. Vision to be the best version of me, in other words look normal.

Man on a mission

The very next day I joined a gym. Didn't know what I was signing up for. For guidance I started watching videos on weight loss and losing chest fat. I kept trying different training programs, which made sense to me without knowing anything about them. All I had was a vision. And I knew my hard work would get me the rewards.

But I was wrong. I did all the wrong things. I had heard of calorie deficit, that one has to eat less and burn more, so I applied it differently. I started starving myself. I would go without eating for hours. I was actually punishing and torturing my body. Thinking that I would lose the unwanted fat in days.

I was impatient, setting myself up for failure. For how long anyone could starve, for how long can you train for hours? Eventually your body will give up and take a toll on you.

I started running for hours. Now the conventional wisdom says that if you burn your calories more than you eat, you will lose weight. I was losing weight but my chest became even saggier. It became so lose that I got even more conscious. Because I was losing fat from my waistline, the chest area started protruding even more. It felt that someone actually pricked a full-blown balloon. In my case the balloon was my belly fat and after excessive cardio, I felt someone took a balloon and had pricked it.

Even though I was losing weight on a consistent basis but the body image of mine was only getting worse. My chest had gone from bad to worse. And I didn't know why I was not losing the fat from my chest. I knew I had to do something different, cardio is not good enough.

So I started researching more. And even approached some of the so called fitness gurus. But most of them recommended steroids which I was not too comfortable injecting. I was of the firm belief that come what may, I would never take anabolic steroids.

I am a believer of hard work and I wanted to be a role model for my younger brother. I didn't want my younger brother to find out that I have taken steroids to transform my body. That's not the example I wanted to set for him. Because I knew if I experiment with anabolic, my younger brother will also think of taking them. And I didn't want to take that road.

The struggle began

I tried every diet in the book. From keto to intermittent fasting. I wanted results. It's not the results but the process. I started to love the process of fat loss and that was a turning point in my life. After that everything appeared so easy and meaningful.

It took me exactly four years to transform myself. From five feet five inches 130 kgs now I am six feet one inch and 80 kgs.

I am a student of fitness. I was learning new ways plus I had no direction, where do I channelize my energy. I kept trying so many new ways and things to transform my body that it actually delayed the results.

Plus the biggest challenge in this journey had been was to keep myself motivated all through out. The problem with us that the moment we see results we get complacent. I remember when I lost ten kgs I was so happy that as a reward I broke my discipline and ended up gaining five kgs back. Consistency is the key.

My journey is not just physical but mental. I felt like giving up so many times. But something kept me going.

What I also realized is that for people with chest fat, cardio is not good enough. That will only help them lose weight. But the real issue of chest fat needs different approach. ON the contrary, if you loose too much weight from the belly, the chest would look even bigger.

The way I attacked this area was very simple

The approach

I introduced strength training into my work outs- Without strength training, or some people would also call it weight training, there is no way you can minimize chest fat. I spent so much time initially running and doing cardio that it made my skin lose and saggy. Strength training will keep your skin elasticity.

The other benefit of strength training is that it will help you lose fat as well. A good strength training session will keep the metabolism elevated for 48 hours. Whereas a cardio session will only burn calories till the time you are performing the exercise. Whatever you do, do not leave strength training.

Strength training won't make you bulky.

For effective fat loss from the chest area, I started training with moderate heavy weights. Now people focus on repetitions. But they don't know that doing heavy weights, you will recruit more muscle fibers and will lose a lot more fat than performing higher repetitions on lightweight.

Diet is the key. Sugar is the enemy of chest fat. Minimizing sugar will have a drastic effect on not just your fat loss goal but also help you lower your chest fat.

Minimizing carbs.

To lower your chest fat, carb intake has to be minimal. Take carbs only before your work out session. Remember people with chest fat gain fat first on their chest, not their stomach. Carbs and starchy food can spell disaster for you. Avoid as much as you can. Utilize the window of carbs viz two hours before the work out or weight training session. This will not only supply you with great energy but also give you a great pump in the gym.

No magic supplements.

There are no magic supplements or pills, which will miraculously change your body in days. It is only your hard work, which will decide the fate of your fat loss journey. Do not invest in any supplements other than whey protein or any mild burners. They will only give you the minor edge but rest it will your effort, which will sail you through.

Live your dreams don't let anyone make you feel uncomfortable about yourself. We all have in us, its just about unleashing the real you. Do it now, its never too late.

Your boobs are bigger than mine

There comes a time in your life when you realize that there is something unusual about the way your body looks especially your chest, because we see actors on television and friends around us having a very normal flat chest.

Then you start asking your parents about this situation. They being your parents will always tell you that it is normal. And if you ignore this, it can turn into something big which can haunt you for the rest of your life. But when your girl friend tells you that your boobs are bigger than mine, that can really take a hit on your ego.

Think about that situation when that happens to anyone. You are a normal sixteen year old who is dating a girl. The other guys are making fun of you chest but you can put up with all that. But when your girl friend also joins hands with them and starts to make fun of you then that can be brutal.

My girlfriend said "your breast is bigger than mine"

This is a story of Ekansh who I met few months ago in my journey of meeting with people with chest fat and how they overcame it.

Ekansh realised he had male boobs when people around him started poking fun and made silly comments about his chest. Some even called it breasts. But he ignored thinking they are just jealous. But when someone makes a comment you do tend to think sometimes is it really the case.

And then when you find something different about yourself than others is when you start questioning yourself. And this is where it all starts.

If you have chest fat or male boobs it is fine, but when people start making fun of it, is when it hits you the most. Ekansh was also one of them. He was very comfortable with his body only when his friends made him realise that what he has is something very weird. This made him extremely conscious about his own body image.

Even his school teachers started pointing out indirectly about his chest fat though in a very subtle way. Teachers, friends, and even relatives saying the same thing, you have male boobs, you are turning into a woman. How would anyone feel?

I became so conscious and uncomfortable about myself that I started covering my body by wearing loose clothes. I always thought people are looking at me and will pass a comment anytime. At one point I got so fat, that I felt the need to tuck my belly fat under my pants, obviously in no time I became a laughing stock of my school, said Ekansh

Needed help

I used to go up to my mother asking her what will it take for me to lose this male boobs. But obviously she would have no answer. All she would say this is baby fat and will go with time.

But I had found a way to hide my boobs by wearing a tight vest underneath my shirt. And every time I would feel my chest is getting loose, I would pull the vest down and tuck it under my pants from below. This became my hack, which I followed for few days but obviously could not last long because bullies catch you.

I used to tighten up my vest so much that my shoulders had marks of the vest. Something like if you wear a bikini and go in the sun. Your whole body will be tanned but the marks of the bikini strap will appear on its own.

My parents didn't really acknowledge that I actually had a problem. They always thought it was baby fat and I am getting conscious for absolutely no reason at all. So I could not even talk to them.

Someone recommended that I should start taking whey proteins, which will help me minimise this chest fat problem of mine. So I really didn't care what was it or what it will do, I only wanted to know the solution to my chest fat. When you are going through a problem you actually don't care about the product but the guaranteed solution from that product. I was told that whey proteins, was that solution.

I remember going up to my father asking him for some money to buy whey proteins. He was so against it that even stopped my gym routine, thinking boys there are recommending me banned substances, which I should stay away from. Indian parents are protective and don't really want to do research when it comes to their kids.

The real trigger point was when I was in my 12th standard. My science teacher was very worried about my chest situation. She had seen me tightening the vest and how I was bullied by other schoolmates during recess. She came up to me and gently told me that I should do something about this issue because you going to college will only invite lot of bullies, which may have an adverse effect on my health. I was happy that at least I got intervention from someone senior who was direct and concerned.

To validate, I even spoke with my cousin brother who was in college. He shared his ragging experience, which gave goose bumps and made me hate myself even more. Some students in colleges despite the anti ragging government clause, rag a lot of freshers, and me being an easy prey, would invite lot of their attention.

The thought of ragging by seniors in college started to scare me. Fed up with the outcome, I even thought of committing suicide. Because I had tried all the exercises in the gym, but got no results. It was cleat to me now that there is no escape. I was so helpless that I can't even describe.

She broke my heart

The good part was that I had a girl in my life that I really liked. I thought she really liked me as a person. So one day, I approached her and asked her to be my girl friend. She said something to me, which changed me as a person.

She said I cannot be with you only because we have too many similarities. I could not really understand what she really meant. I asked her what does she mean by similarities. She said you also have boobs. On the contrary your boobs are even bigger than mine.

This comment changed me as a person. I really didn't know how to react to this but deep down I made up mind, that come what may I would do something to prove her wrong. I gave myself a target which is to change my body in six months and put a body shot of mine with a caption tagging her " yes we do have similar bodies".

Obviously I could not achieve my goal in three months. It took me almost three years to transform myself. And that journey has been so rewarding. I used to be a boy who liked a girl but after transforming myself I became a man who now had so many girls liking him.

What did Ekansh do to transform his body and minimise his chest fat.

Guidance. For any transformation, it is extremely important to have a mentor who can guide you with your goal. In Ekansh case, he found his mentor, Gurmeet Dua, who guided him with his fitness-training plan but most importantly he taught him how to manage his food intake.

Managing macros

The day you understand how to calculate your macronutrients, body transformation will be a piece of cake. How much food one should eat and at what time, his mentor only focused on teaching him the science of calculating macros. It is very easy. Just start writing whatever you are eating and Google the rest. For example, if you ate two rotis, Google how many calories two rotis would have. Google will give you an eighty percent accurate number. Gradually start writing your daily calories intake. The idea is to know your numbers. In life everything can be broke down into numbers because numbers don't lie.

Supplements

People don't get it. They think supplements can replace our actual food. But there is a reason they are called supplements. They are meant to be supplemented along with their diet. Don't try to replace the diet with supplements. Ekansh took only three products, which included whey proteins, BCAA and glutamine for recovery. All the products are natural and have no illegal or banned substances.

Training

He trained almost three hours seven days a week. Obviously he had a point to prove. But training without purpose is no use. Just like you need a goal in your career, similarly you also need a vision for your fitness. Always ask yourself these questions

- **Why are you training**
- **What will happen if you get the results?**
- **Who are you doing this for**

Answer these questions for yourself but most importantly remember you are doing this for yourself no one else.

I was desperate

I see the desperation of so many boys trying to get rid of their man boobs. I have been there but not at the cost of your health. As part of my interview process, I came across men who have tried all kinds of dangerous substances and steroids to minimise their chest fat. So much so that some of them have even compromised on their health and were hospitalised for days.

Rajat is one such guy, who I met recently. He was a super active guy and very fit. He had a perfect body if someone were to see it with his clothes on. But the moment he would take his shirt off, it would be a different site.

Rajat was a classic victim of chest fat. He was fat in his early childhood and with his sheer hard work had lost considerable amount of fat from his body. But the chest fat was stubborn and refused to go for years. This stubborn chest fat gave him nightmares. Can you imagine having a decent physique but a out of shape chest area.

His chest area gave an illusion of a female breast. He was adamant to fix this issue. And then he started researching on the internet on the cure for male boobs. The only cure for male boobs is surgery but with a strong training and diet plan, chest fat can be minimised to quite an extent.

And while researching he came across some anabolic steroids, which claimed to Harden the body and get you in your dream shape. And we all know forbidden fruit is always tempting. He researched some more and started talking to his gym trainers about them.

He got all kind of feedback. Some told him its safe he should give a shot while some stopped him from taking them. But he was hell bent to try them. So he finally ordered from one of the trainers.

What he got was some pills. He obviously didn't know how to take them or the correct dosage. So he experimented with his dosages by googling everything. This can be a very dangerous drill. Everything was working fine. He was beginning to see the results and was somewhat pleased with them.

He was getting impatient and wanted to speed up the process. So he increased the dosage. And within when he took the pill, within few hours, he felt palpitation in his heart, which he had never experienced. He went online and read the side effect of the pill. This side effect was mentioned.

So he didn't pay that much heed to it. But within minutes he was finding it difficult to breathe. So much so that he had to call his friend to take him to hospital. When the friend arrived in his house, he was found on the floor unconscious.

Immediately he was taken to the nearby hospital and was diagnosed with heart attack. He was lucky to have called his friend at the right time. Any delay would have spelled disaster. But he survived.

It took him weeks to recover from this medical trauma. And he decided to stay away from all this. He is now comfortable with his body and has accepted that no one is perfect. Just don't try to look perfect, because that perfection can cost you your life.

Deep message isn't.

The chest fat surgery alternative

In this section, I want to make you meet someone who actually underwent chest fat removal surgery. He lived with it for over ten years. And when he had enough, he decided to have the surgery done.

The road to surgery was not easy. He not only had to convince his parents but also himself for this medical treatment of going under the knife. What prompted him to go for a surgery because surgery is always the last option.

I spoke with Angad and he shared his journey.

Chest fat is something you realise when you see yourself in the mirror. You somehow know that there is something unusual about that chest area but don't really know what to do especially in the young age. You may ask your parents but most of the Indian parents will ignore this conversation let alone help you find a solution. They want to ignore because they don't want you to start thinking that you are not normal.

This is the same case with Angad, he knew he had some fat on his chest which made him stand out from the other boys of his age. He was only fourteen years old, when he first saw his chest fat taken a shape of male boobs.

He started questioning himself on why is it happening to him only. Why the other boys have no such issue? Their chest appears to be absolutely fine. He started researching on the Internet. That's where he figured out a term called gynecomastia, an enlarged breast syndrome in men, which can only be fixed by a surgery.

Disheartening

Now this can be heartbreaking for anyone who is desperate to find a solution for chest fat. I was devastated to know the treatment for chest fat. Obviously the thought of telling my parents that I want to be operated to remove my male boobs, was very embarrassing. So I decided to find a fix on my own.

I was hell bent to figure out a way around this. Within three months of knowing this, I joined a gym. I must have been in ninth standard. And without wasting any time I started asking al the trainers the solution to my chest fat problem. And some recommended a quick solution in a form of anabolics. I barely knew anything about anabolic steroids, all I was told that it will help me minimise the fat.

And in no time I had access to those dangerous drugs. There are two ways to take anabolic steroids. One is the oral way, which comes in pills, and the other is through injectables. Oral is considered to be more dangerous since it takes time to break into the body thus stressing the liver to work extra hard.

And because I was too young, these drugs started working on my body. I lost considerable amount of weight and started looking in shape. But the reason why I started taking these drugs in the first place saw no results. My chest fat stayed where it was. So now my chest was standing out even more, a lean stomach with a fatty chest. This made the situation even worse and the only option I felt that time was to leave this gym.

But deep down, I was so desperate to fix this that I could go to any extreme. So this time I joined a new gym with new set of trainers. And trainers in this new gym recommended me injectables. Unlike many other fifteen to sixteen year olds, my goal was not to be a fitness model or an athlete but to just minimise my male boobs.

Felt side effects

I could feel the side effects including palpitations and heart beats but I let go thinking this is a part of my fitness journey. I will put my body through anything so long I can achieve my goal.

The worse part about all this I could not even tell all this at home. What would I tell that I am doing steroids to fix my chest fat. I hid all this from my parents and that guilt was killing me from within.

Silver lining

But then I had a trainer who knew my situation and decided to help me. He gave me a steroid cycle, which as per him would solve my problem. I kept taking shots after shots for six weeks. But my chest fat remained the same. So I asked myself! Is this it? I cannot fix this problem of mine despite using all the drugs and steroids in the world.

I gave up on everything, even left my training. I didn't train for over two years. My parents got worried that the guy who was training for seven days has not even stepped a foot in the gym for weeks, there is got to be something wrong.

And then I confronted them and shared my situation. Luckily they understood what I was going through and decided to help me and take me to a doctor. And even the doctor recommended surgery.

The surgery

The surgery was not painful. The doctor told me that they would prick both my nipples and extract the fat from there. The thought of it was scary but I was only visualising my chest, which would be normal now so I sailed through.

The surgery only took few hours. I went in the morning and was home in the evening. I remember seeing my chest fat for the last time and even said goodbye to them. And promised myself that I will never ever see it again.

After the surgery ended, I was so happy. I felt lighter and the best part, I could wear anything I wanted to. Plus I didn't have to put my body through any of that risk of steroids and drugs. That was quite a relief.

After a few days, I realised I was a totally different guy. My confidence had skyrocketed. I went to my favourite retail clothing store and picked up the clothes which I could never wear due to my chest fat. I now wear them with swag and confidence.

I may have paid Rs. 1.3 lacs for the surgery but the confidence I have acquired is valuable cannot be quantified.

99% of all such surgeries are painless and safe but exceptions are always there.

Anything can get you your confidence back, and you can afford then you should not wait and get the surgery done.

But if you are one of those who would work extremely hard and not give up and get the results, that option always exist.

Now that's the call you have to take.

My learnings

In my journey of losing chest fat, I discovered the real me, and have learnt a lot in the process which I would I now be sharing with you.

There is no such thing as spot reduction

I always had a goal of losing chest fat ignoring that in itself won't be possible. Why because spot reduction as a concept doesn't really work. Which means we cannot just cut fat from one body part, it has to be holistic. For example, if you are starting out your journey to lose chest fat, don't just focus on minimising fat from your chest, look at it as a whole. By focusing only on chest fat you are setting yourself for failure. I shared all the stories of all the people in this book, all of them had one thing to say, I wanted to get rid of my male boobs. But no one really focused on lowering body fat.

Once your body fat goes down, so will your chest fat. Now this is a million dollar learning, which no one ever shared with me. It took me twelve years to figure this one out.

Supplementation

I know I would disappoint you on this but please note there is no such thing a s miracle product. You will be tempted to try out many products all claiming to help you lose that chest fat but those are all gimmicks and marketing propagandas.

In my journey I must have tried at least a hundred products, spent lacs of rupees on supplements, which never really worked. All these products were bought out of desperation with the intent of losing fat overnight. Desperation calls for desperate measures, but don't be instinctive and save your money.

So what

In this section I want to share something very personal. I know ninety percent of people reading this book may not be successful at minimising their chest fat. And trust me it is not your fault. It takes a lot to push yourself out of our comfort zone.

But I want you to remember something. It is ok if you can't fix your chest fat, it is ok if you have male boobs, it is ok if people make fun of you, they anyways will. Even if you fix your chest fat, you will still have many areas in your body, which you would not like and would want to change. Life is like that; God keeps us busy with new goals and projects. But don't torture yourself. Just accept that and get comfortable with that notion.

Love yourself

We all have weaknesses and it takes a strong person to accept those weaknesses and work towards them. Even if you fail in your attempt to combat chest fat, my only request to you is don't give up. Keep fighting. I fought for over twelve years before I finally got comfortable with my body. To be honest, all we need is a mindset to be comfortable in our skin, which I find the hardest.

We are so obsessed with the perfect bodies we see on movies and television that it builds that pressure on us to look in a certain way.

Let me share a secret with you.

The Secret

We all see the actors on television and movies. As per us, they are perfect, right? We see their cover shots in the magazines and we think, damn they have a perfect skin, perfect abs and great hair. But let me tell you something.

There is more to what we see. Those body shots that you see undergo a lot of retakes. The perfect body that you see is build in weeks only to look perfect so that you go and watch the movie. Actors are entertainers and they are getting paid to entertain you. They need to look good because that's their occupational hazard.

But the problem is when I see young boys start following them and start working out the way they have been training by watching their YouTube videos or interviews. It is a problem because you are only seeing ten minutes of information of what they are sharing, you have no visibility or proof in what they say holds true or not.

Plus these actors are surrounded by good trainers, dietitians and doctors to medically supervise them, 24x7. Most of us don't have access to such knowledge or food to get to our results. So idolising actors for their bodies is not a good idea. Idealise their journey and how they made it, idealise their body of work not just their bodies. And yes, even actors have weak body parts, which the camera hides.

Don't hate yourself

I get it I have been there. All this time in the last ten to twelve years I hated my body and the way I looked. Somehow my eyes always saw chest fat in the mirror. And I could never get used to this self-image. Resulting in hating myself for this.

I even blamed my genetics. But that's the easiest thing to do. With that mentality, no wonder I never got results. Results started coming in the day I realised I am not supposed to be perfect. Actually no one is perfect. No one has a perfect body. We all have some flaws, which we are constantly trying to hide from others.

The day I accepted myself the way I was, my life changed. I am by no means implying that you should start living with chest fat for the rest of your life. I started loving the process of getting to my dream body. I visualised how I would want to look like.

There is a section in this book where I have told you to start visualising. Negativity is contagious and will drown you in your own life sorrows. My mentor shared something with me, which will give you some perspective.

Even though we don't have a perfect body but think how healthy we all are.

What is the point of having perfect body with abs and ripped chest but at the cost of high blood pressure or any lifestyle disease? Just because someone looks fit doesn't necessarily means he is healthy. I have seen the fittest man who doesn't look perfect and I have seen the guy who looks perfect is the most unfit and healthy. And this thought got into my head.

I realised I can't torture my body and put so many unwanted drugs and products into it that ruins my inner health. Focus on good health not aesthctics. This is the notion I have been living with for years now. And believe me it has changed me as a human being.

Start imagining your life without chest fat. And it starts from there. I know you would say that Tarun how is this possible? I see that part of my body every minute of the day. But that's what conditioning is about. Fitness is not about how you look but how stable is your head. How do you take control of your mind and channelize it towards your goal.

I have been practicing this for years and will now share how you can also do the same and be the best version of who you are. Let me tell you this requires discipline and commitment to a lifestyle. Lets start.

Life without chest fat

I am sure if you are reading this, you are struggling with your body image. And that is why I have introduced this section. As I shared in my previous chapters, we all have a weak or rather a lagging body part, which we hate. But that hate should only be about that particular body part, which should drive you to insane to fix it.

But the opposite happens. That lagging body part makes us hate ourselves. At least it has been in my case. Because of my chest I hated my life. So much so I went into depression and at some point thought of killing myself. I thought of myself as a victim. A victim who was always questioning God on why he made me this way.

- **Why do I have male boobs.**
- **Why can't I be normal**
- **Why can't I wear normal clothes like others**
- **Why do I have to hide my chest**
- **Why do people make fun of me**
- **Why don't I have the confidence I should**

- **Why can't I wear clothes I want to wear**
- **Why do I have to wear what hides my chest fat**
- **Why do I have to wear a vest or an inner**
- **Why can't I go swimming without having to worry about my chest fat**
- **Why can't I change my clothes in the locker with the rest of the boys**
- **Why, why and some more whys...**

I am sure you also have the same why which you are looking an answer for. But let me tell you something. The answer lies within you. You just need to rewire your brain, the way I did. Here is what I did.

Before I get started, I will not give you anything philosophilcal but something which I have tried one myself. Here it is.

Time out 15 minutes everyday

I know you are busy and you barely take out time for your work out. But I am sure you can squeeze fifteen minutes everyday for the activity I am about to share.

Every day for fifteen minutes, I want you to close your eyes. Be with me, I know where I am going with this. In these fifteen minutes, just focus on your dream body. Visualise how you want to look like. Believe me, most of us don't even know how we want to look like if were to get to our goal. It is because we don't even know our goal.

This was the problem I was going through. I had boarded a bus but didn't really knew where it was heading. But I knew I am on the way to something. What was missing in my journey was destination.

So let me ask you what is your destination. Do you even know where you are headed? You may have all the answers when I ask you about your career goals but when it comes to your health, you would be clueless. Even I was. I had absolutely no idea how I should look like. All I cared about was losing chest fat.

Our mind needs a goal for it to deliver. Go back to your school days. You always had a goal didn't you either to pass the tests or to top the class. In your professional life to be a doctor or in a corporate set up, get your next promotion or a raise. This is how our brain is wired. It works on targets and goals. Now imagine you went to school with no goal to pass the exams or no goal to become a doctor.

This is how I was living with chest fat with absolute no goal of my ideal body. Unless you see yourself in the doctor uniform, you would never be able to become a doctor. Similarly if you don't see yourself in the shape you want to be in, you will never be able to get to that shape.

In these fifteen minutes downtime, I want you to visualise that goal of yours. Do it everyday. Remember the training plan I shared with you is just a tool to get you close to your goal.

What is your purpose–why are you doing this?

Now before you get down and start visualizing your goal, you need to find an answer to this question which I am about to ask you.

Why do you want to lose your chest fat or transform your body? How will your life change when you will lose your chest fat or get a dream body. Now most of you would have an easy answer such as I want to feel good or look good etc. But that why won't be good enough for you to get to your goal.

You need to find a deeper why. I will tell you what has been my why.

The reason I wanted to lose my chest fat so that I could live a life of my own dreams which I had to compromise for these years. I want that confidence which would propel me to drive forward in life which has been holding me back for years. Getting rid of chest fat will give me a sense of accomplishment that I can do anything in life, which will help me achieve far bigger goals.

These were my biggest two mistakes

1. I didn't have a goal

2. I didn't know my purpose

Goal you will find by visualising your dream body and purpose you will find by answering why you want to lose chest fat and how will it change you as a person.

Transformation is a mental game

Lot of us think transforming our body is a physical task but you would be surprised to know that ninety percent is a mental game. Your mind drives all the effort, which the body responds to. Dont believe me!

- **Think about the last fitness program you followed and could not continue?**

- **Think about why you didn't feel like Training everyday even though your body is not tired**

- **Why you always give reasons and excuses to skip the work out.**

Let me tell you why. Your mind is playing with your body and calling the shots. Sooner you realise the faster you will transform. So how do you take charge of your mind. Now this is a whole new exercise. Monks and sadhus have been practicing for years to take control of their thoughts and some of them have been successful.

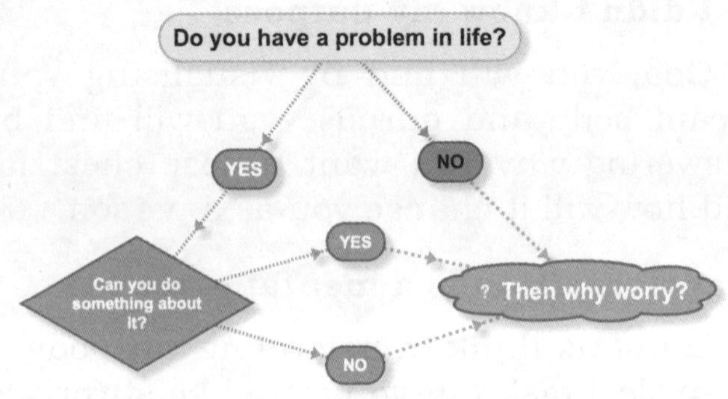

I found Gaur Gopal Prabhu very practical who helped me a lot in channelizing my thoughts. I am sharing his favourite chart, which he has been preaching the world on. It's called "why worry"

Why worry concept is very simple. Ask yourself just one question

"Do you have a problem in life?

If the answer is yes, follow it up with another question

Can you do something about it

If the answer is yes

Then why do you need to worry, when you already have a solution

If the answer is no

If its not in your hands, how will worrying help

I applied the same concept in my chest fat journey:

Do I have a problem

Yes I do, its chest fat

Can I do something about it.

Yes I can, by applying training, nutrition and supplementation to get to my results.

Then why and what the hell am I worried about.

I am going to ask you the same question now

DO you have a problem

If you have a chest fat problem

I am giving you the solution to fix it.

If you don't want to follow it and let it be a problem, still its fine

Why worry.

This why worry gave me a whole new direction. I stopped having unwanted negative thoughts in my head. and focused on the real task

You are your biggest enemy

You are your biggest enemy, and there is a reason why I say it. All these years you have been hating yourself with the way you look. Exactly what I was doing. Torturing my body by consuming all the products and substances to minimise chest fat.

If I loved my body-

1. **I would not have abused it**
2. **I would not have hated it**
3. **I would not have had any body shaming thoughts**
4. **I would have stood up my ground**
5. **I would not have let anyone bully me**
6. **I would have replied all the bullies back who made fun of my chest**
7. **I would not have cried at home**

So what does that make me–My own worst enemy.

So everyday I was feeding the enemy within who always pulled me down, kept me miles away from my goals. This enemy cultivated negative thoughts in my head that I am good for nothing and can never get rid of chest fat. This enemy instilled in me that I have to live with chest fat all my life. This enemy made me his slave.

What if you can't fix your chest fat

If I were to tell you that despite you try everything from training, diet to supplementation and still for some reason you may not be able to minimise your chest fat, what would you do?

Will you give up hope or continue to try

Let me give you a third option- Get comfortable with your discomfort.

Yes you heard me right! There can be a possibility that you may have to live with your chest fat for the rest of your life. Will you be depressed for the rest of your life. Will you give up on your life. Will you go back to your shell and not socialise at all. Will you continue to hate yourself.

Obviously you would not! Remember we only have one life to live. SO what I you can't fix your chest fat. Now you would think, that Tarun can say all that he can, because he has already found a solution to his problem. But that is not the case. I may have fixed my chest fat but most importantly I have fixed this problem of chest fat in my head.

I have become so comfortable with myself that it doesn't affect me what people say about my body. Let me tell you chest fat can only be fixed with surgery. With my program you can minimise it by 70-80 percent, which I managed to do.

Coming back to my question " what if you can't fix this problem?. Here is what I will recommend that you should do.

Live your life

Your life can't revolve around fixing this problem. You have people around you who have been of great support to you. They need attention from you. And you being stuck with your problem will only affect your relationship with them. Spend time with them.

I have been so stuck with my depression related to my chest fat that I almost forget to live my life. My life revolved around finding solutions to fix my chest fat. I forgot that there is a beautiful world outside my problem, which needs to be explored.

I will urge you; don't get caught up with your problem. Even if you manage to solve this problem, you will always find another one to work on. Problems are endless, but solutions lie with us.

If you remember the previous section where I asked you why do you want to minimise your chest fat. That is the why and the purpose to stay happy and be happy with your body.

The idea is not to stop training, not to get distracted by your goal. But if the results don't come easy, just stay on track. It is fine sometimes to have a cheat meal. Give yourself a treat and a pat on the back for being disciplined.

Sometimes our body needs a metabolism reset. Which means if you have the same thing for a continuous period of time, the results would stop and stagnate. That is the time to introduce and shock your body with new food items for it to respond.

That is why a cheat meal is so important. Not only it is a reward for your hard work but also it is a great shock therapy. Eat the food you love and instead of harming you it will only do good to you. But remember cheat meal is meant ot be earned.

Don't reward yourself too much. If your boss or coach starts telling you good Job too often it would lose the impact. So don't make it a daily ritual. Reserve it and earn it.

In the end, all I would tell you is don't torture yourself. Keep working towards your goal to fix your chest fat. It is ok if you fail, but remember you need to be healthy. Put your health first before anything else. All the best.

WEEK 1

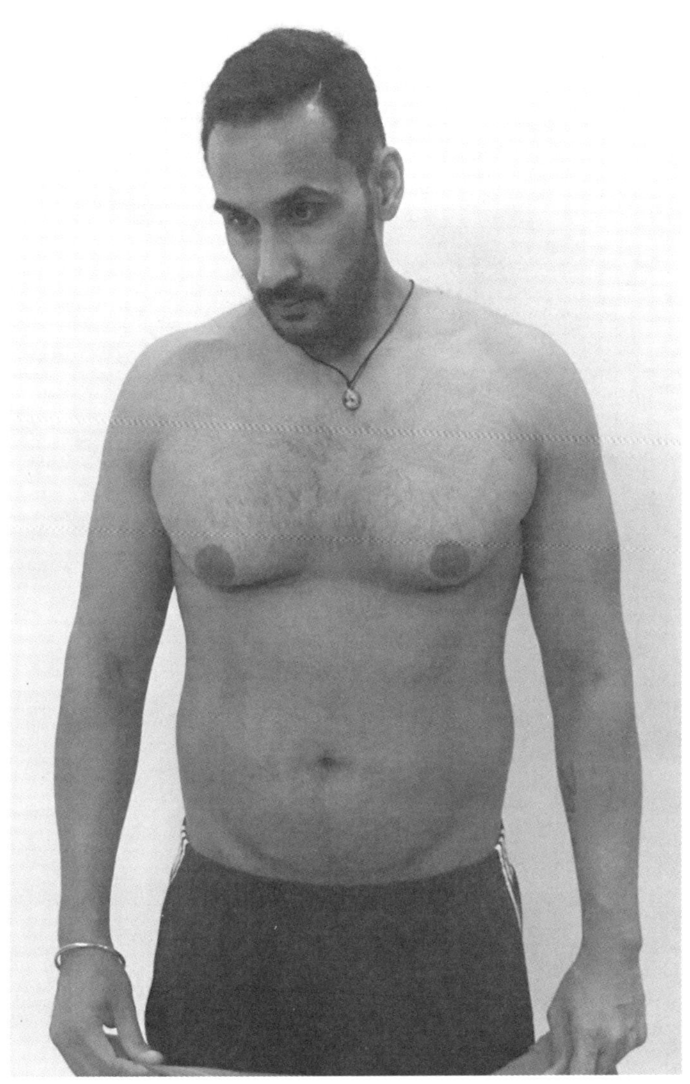

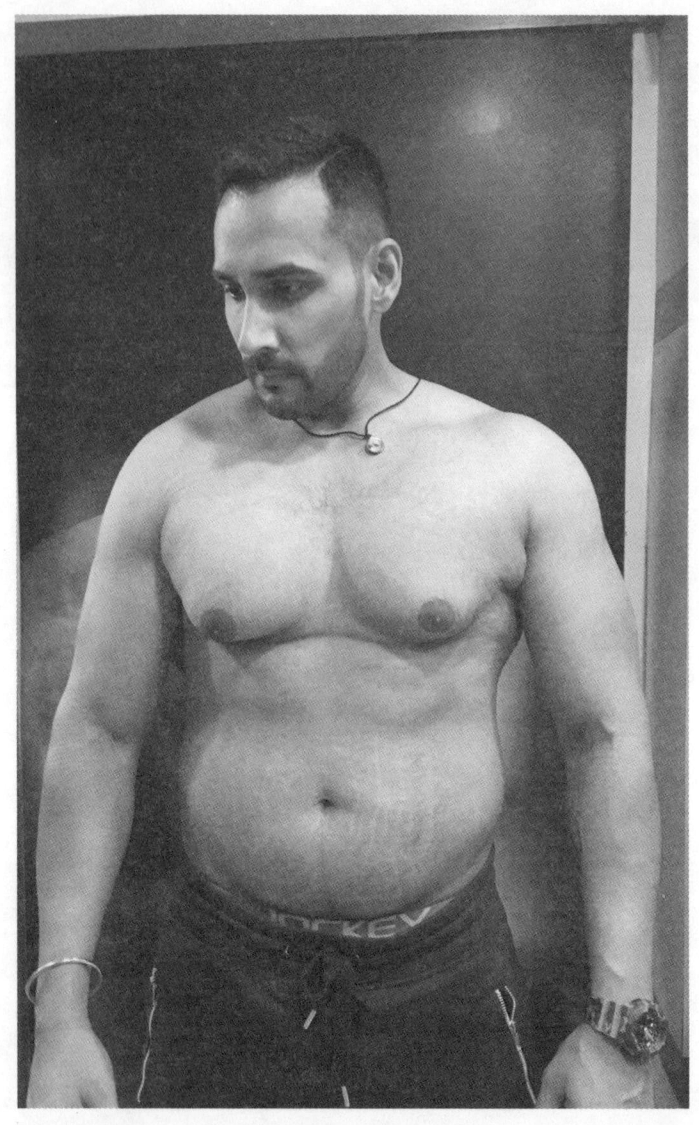

WEEK 2

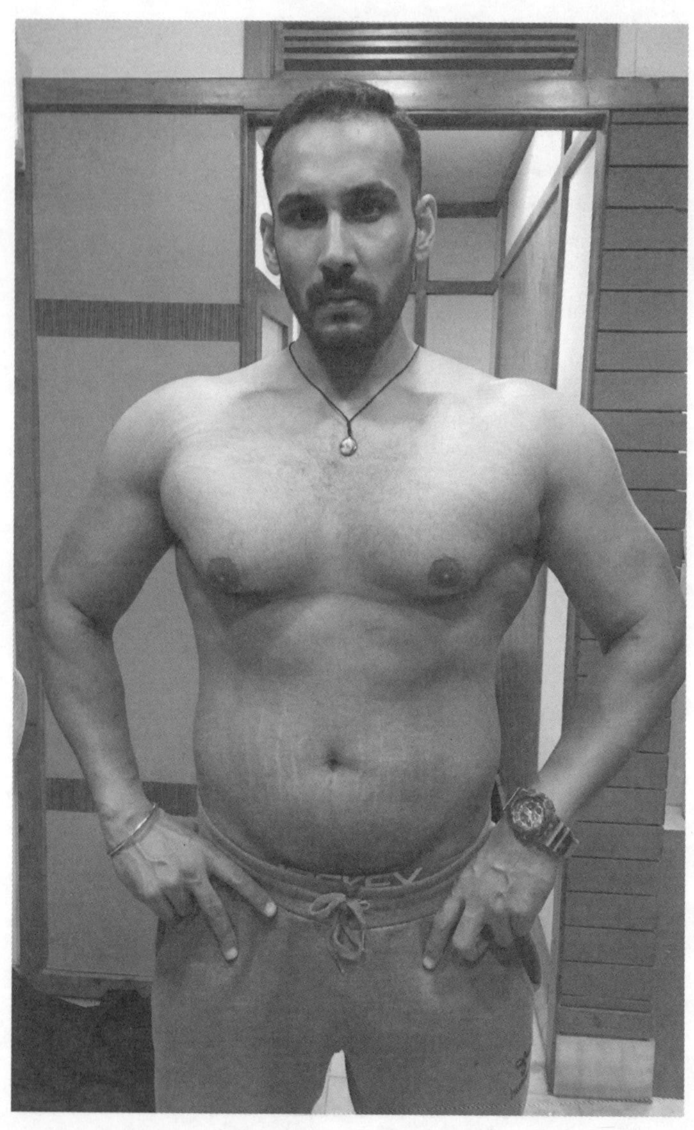

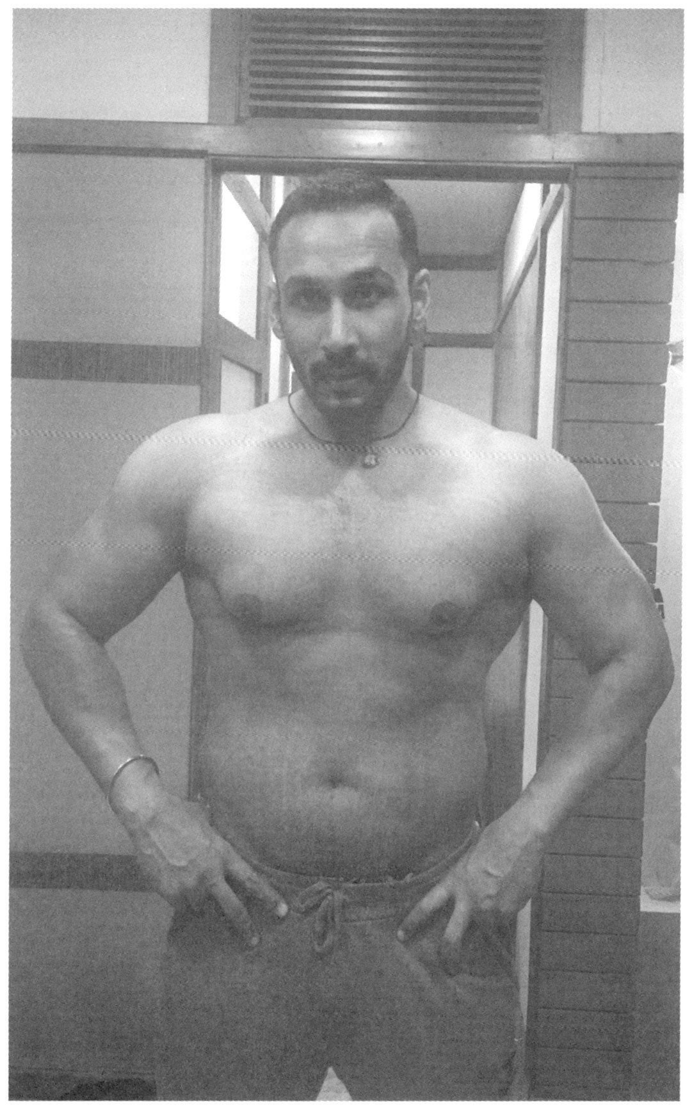

WEEK 3

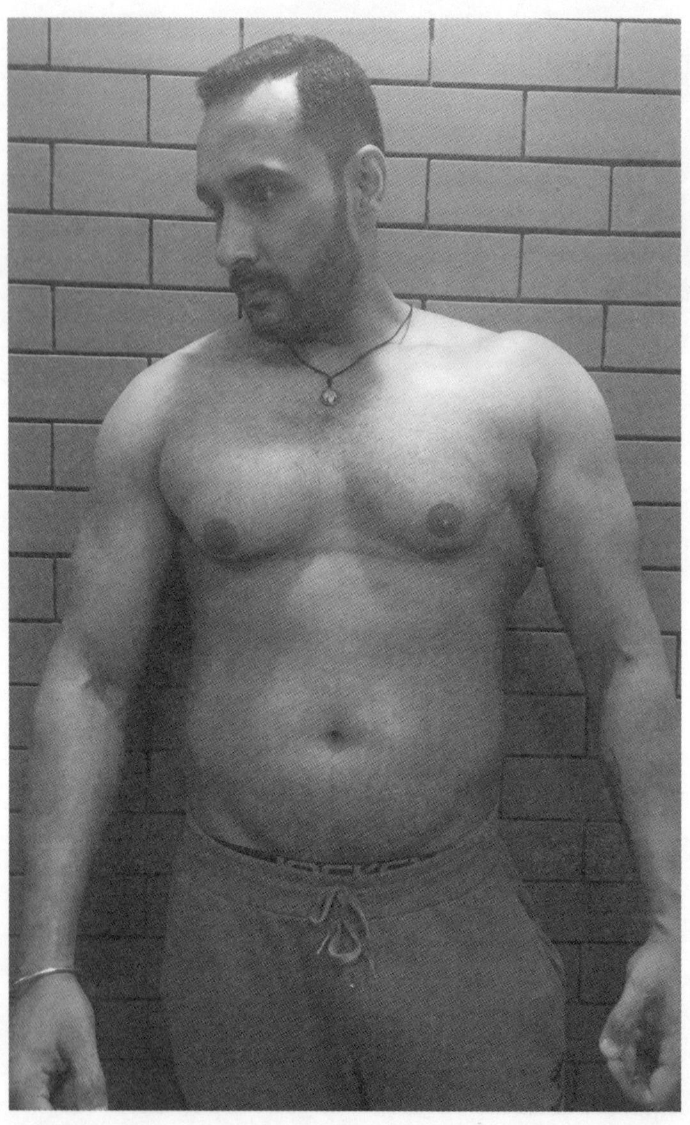

WEEK 4

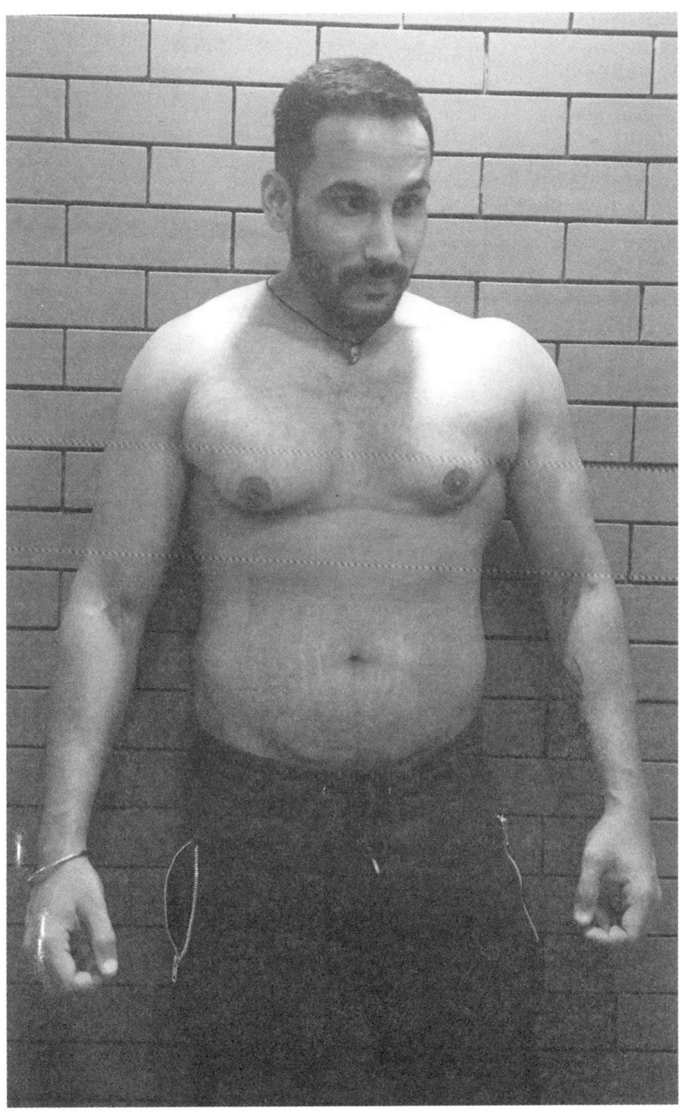

WEEK 5

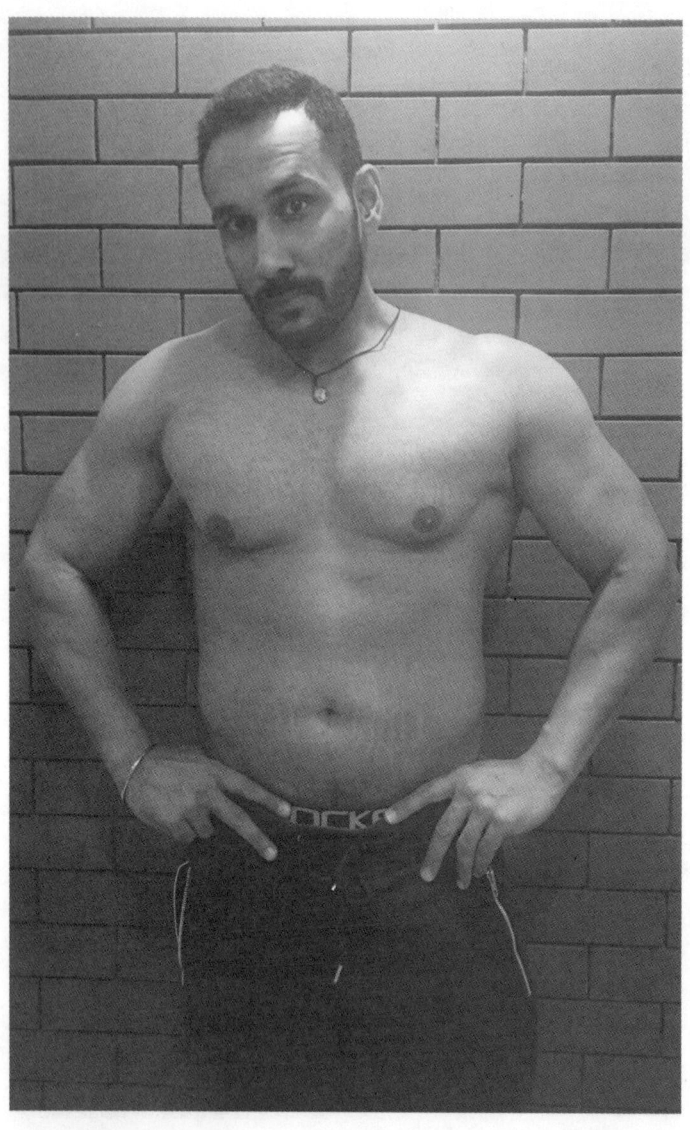

WEEK 6

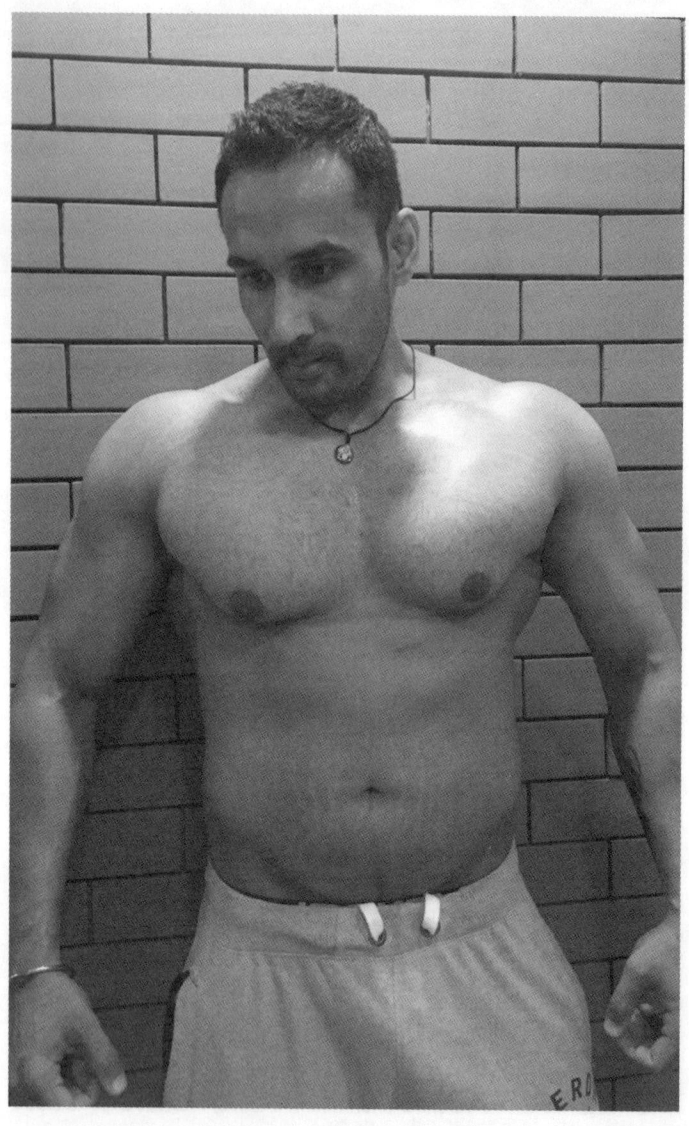

WEEK 7

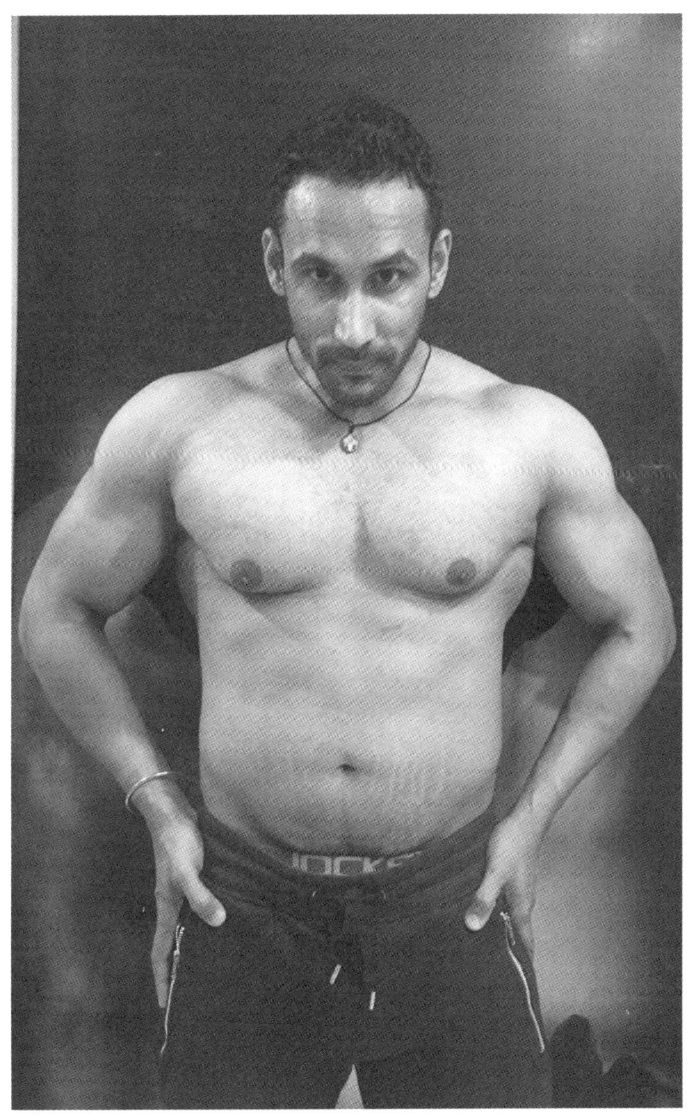

WEEK 8

WEEK 9

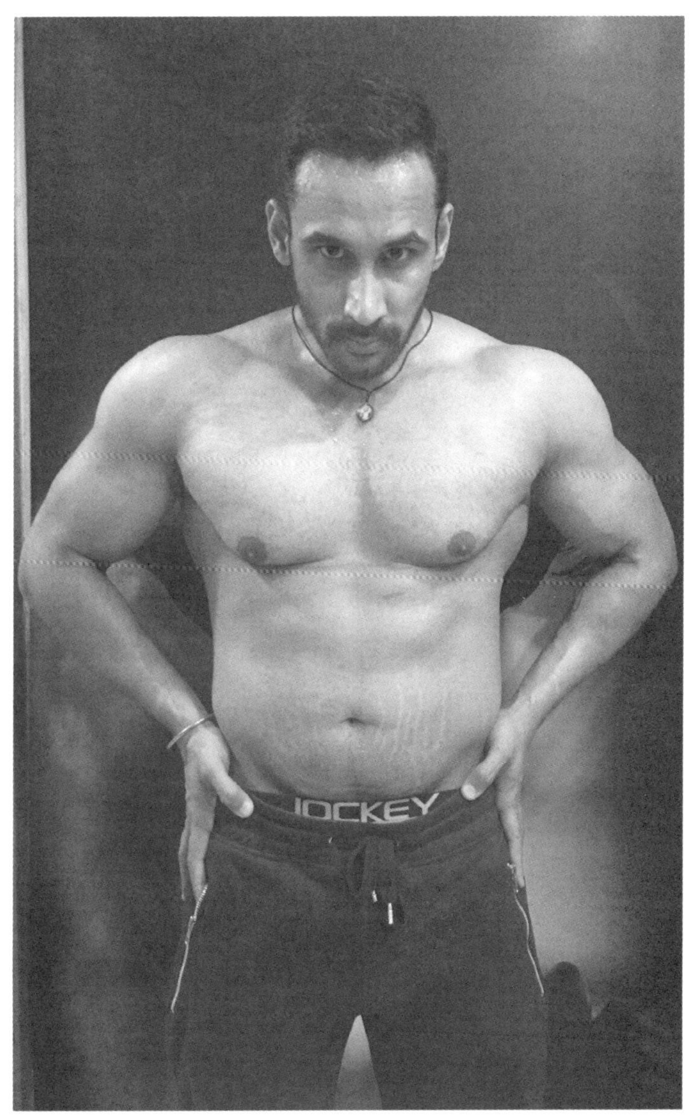

WEEK 10

WEEK 11

WEEK 12

DAY 4
DAY 75
TARUN GILL
FIXING CHEST FAT FOR LIFE
www.chestfatremoval.com

PHOTOGRAPHY
VARUN TYAG

Day 55
Day 1

ON A DIET
FAT% 15
WEIGHT 77 KG
EATING THREE TIMES MORE
FAT% 10%
WEIGHT 85 KGS

55 DAYS JOURNEY

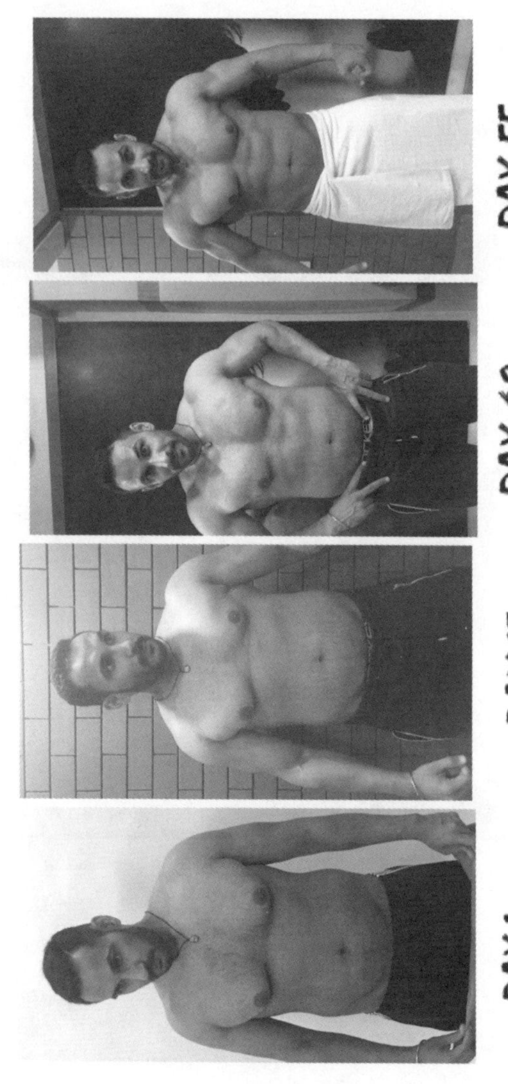

DAY 1 DAY 15 DAY 40 DAY 55

HOW TO BOOST YOUR TESTOSTERONE IN A WEEK GUARANTEED

INTRODUCTION

Lets face it, every man in any part of the world is obsessed with increasing his testosterone levels. What can he do to increase it naturally! Some even go down the route of increasing it artificially with the help of pills claiming to work like magic. There have been many studies on the role of testosterone in a man's body and almost have one common finding, viz testosterone works like an oxygen for men, the more he has it the better he feels.

Which, I think its true at least for me. As India's leading fitness influencer, I get this question a lot from people asking me what can they do to increase their testosterone levels. Some of them are only in their early twenties.

I am nineteen and I feel my testosterone levels are low, because I don't feel like masturbating or having sex.

I am twenty-six, newly married for two months, and I cant perform which is giving me nightmares.

I am in my late thirties, and I have lost the urge to have sex, I feel extremely weak and lethargic.

This is not uncommon these days, considering the life style we all have. Almost every day I am bombarded with such questions, so I thought why not just answer it for everyone, even for people who are embarrassed to ask such questions.

This book will help you understand:

- The symptoms of low-test levels.
- Causes which leads to it
- Training which you can do to boost
- Food you can eat to accelerate your body's test levels
- Supplements, which you may want to add to speed up the process.

Let me clarify I am not a sexologist or a doctor, but a certified fitness and nutrition expert and my advise will be based on my experience and science of fitness. I will try to keep it as simple as I can so everyone can understand without the use of any technical jargon.

So lets get started.

What is testosterone?

Test is predominantly male hormone, which is associated with sex drive and libido. Even though women ovaries make testosterone but that is in very limited quantity. The production of test in males typically starts when they are twelve years old and gradually dips after age thirty.

Test levels take a hit and drop every year after a man turns thirty.

If the test levels dip after a man turns thirty, why is it that men who are hardly nineteen years old face the problem of low libido? Lets address this in the next segment.

Do you have low test- testing test?

How do you know if your test levels are low? Even though low libido itself is quite a sign of low test levels, but it is always recommended to get the medical test done for your testosterone.

A blood test can easily gauge and determine your existing test levels. There is lot of test floating in your bloodstream, which will tell you the current levels.

What is the normal test range?

The normal range of testosterone for most healthy male adults is between 250 and 1100 ng/dL.

A. Vermeleun (1996)

Age	Total Testosterone (ng/dL)	Free Testosterone (ng/dL)	SHBG (nmol/L)
25-34	617	12.3	35.5
35-44	668	10.3	40.1
45-54	606	9.1	44.6
55-64	562	8.3	45.5
65-74	524	6.9	48.7
75-84	471	6.0	51.0
85-100	376	5.4	65.9

How to fix low test medically?

People with low testosterone levels often go for Test replacement therapy (TRT). You would be surprised, that most of the bodybuilders across the globe are on TRT. There is nothing wrong with TRT it is just a treatment.

Just like people get treated for any other problem, men experiencing low test usually opt for TRT. If you feel that your sex drive is affecting your life and mental health, TRT could be the option you can explore.

What is the TRT treatment?

Testosterone Replacement Therapy (TRT), is nothing but a hormone replacement therapy in which medicines are prescribed to bring your test levels back to normal 250-1100 ng/dl.

What are different types of TRT?

There are many types of TRT including test patches and gels, which you can rub on your shoulders or stomach. But primarily TRT would involve artificial test injections (steroids) given at regular intervals supervised by doctors. Once the test levels come back to normal, the dose of these synthetic testosterones is tapered off.

Some would call TRT a legal way to take anabolic steroids to enhance muscle growth. That is one of the reasons why TRT is such a controversial yet debatable topic across the globe.

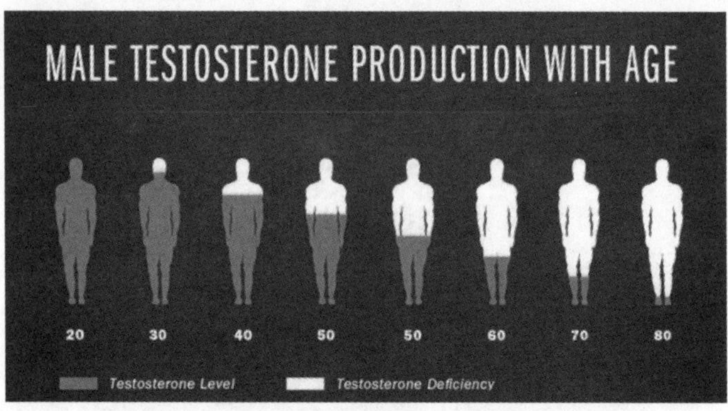

Will it be safe to call TRT same as anabolic steroids usage?

The answer is no! Because bodybuilders and athletes take anabolic steroids to enhance their sports performance, while increasing their test levels to abnormal heights, which is dangerous in the long term. Where as TRT is being prescribed and is medically monitored to bring back a man's test level to his normal range.

Test injections in TRT:

Doctors usually prescribe, two different forms of Test injections which includes

- Enanthate
- Cypionate

What is usually the dose of test in TRT?

This depends from person to person depending on their current test levels. It usually varies from 50-150 mgs every ten days.

Now that you have a fair bit of idea of test and TRT, lets move on and understand what are the causes of low-test levels in males.

Causes of low-test levels

Having low-test levels is not uncommon these days. It's the sedentary lifestyle, which is what leads to decline in the test levels. But there are many other factors too. Lets look at them

Medications

Blood thinners, or medicines which are used to lower blood pressure, can significantly bring down men test levels. These medications can have an effect on erections and even ejaculation. If you are experiencing low libido levels, it could be because these medicines.

Stress

Higher levels of stress are responsible for lowering your sex drive. This stress will only give you sleepless nights but also will spell disaster for your sex life.

Depression

We have been a victim of depression, especially when we go through a break up or a loss of loved ones. Depression as a medical problem is treatable but one of the ways to treat this is by prescribing anti-depressants medicines. And these medicines may have an effect on the libido levels. Therefore it is very important to get the dosage of such medicines right by speaking to your doctor.

Sleep patterns

If you have trouble falling asleep in the night or your sleep pattern is disturbed, this could spell disaster for your sex life. I can give you my own example! There was a time in my life when I had trouble sleeping in the night. Could be because I felt I was more productive in the night to finish my work. But as this became a habit, I realized that not sleeping in the night, lead to abdomen fat and low sex drive. And that gave me stress, considering I am in the business of fitness.

After three months of self-searching, I finally fixed this habit of sleeping in the night and within two weeks; I not only was losing that fat but also felt a lot better mentally.

Historically and biologically, our body's clock shuts down in the night, which prompts us to sleep, and we usually dodge that resulting in low libido most of the times too.

Age

Age is an acceptable reason for your low-test levels. As described in my previous segment, men libido levels decrease after they turn thirty. And every year, the test levels go down. This is the universal truth and you cannot change it, but yes you can delay it. We will see it in our next segment.

SYMPTOMS OF LOW TEST LEVELS

Low sex drive

One of the obvious signs of low-test levels is the low libido, inability to perform in bed. This is self-explanatory and we will go in detail.

Hair loss

This has been my experience, during the time when my sleep pattern was disturbed which eventually lowered my libido. I did notice considerable amount of hair loss in that period, which I thought was due to weather change or impurity of water. If you start experiencing hair loss, all of a sudden, backed with low libido, this is quite a sign.

Body fat

This is a classic example of hormonal imbalance. Going back to childhood, which I also shared in my other book "How I fixed my chest fat" this imbalance lead to increased estrogen, the female hormone, in my body causing extreme amount of body and abdomen fat, which I struggled for almost fifteen years to fix.

If you are experiencing this increased body fat, low-test levels could be the reason.

Gyno

The hormonal imbalance can also lead to gyno, development of breast tissue in males. This is also one of the key signs of low-test levels, which needs to be immediately addressed.

Loss of Muscle mass

Since test is responsible for building muscles in males, the lowered test levels, will lead to loss of muscle mass. If you find yourself putting on weight and losing muscle mass and at times feeling jaded and tired, this in itself is a sign that your test levels are lowered. And you need to get your blood test done to get your level checked.

Now comes the interesting part.

How can you increase the test levels in a week? No I will not recommend TRT. What I am about to share with you is the tried and tested way, it has worked on more than one hundred clients of my clients.

Here is how.

Training

When you experience the low-test levels, all you need to do is pull yourself up and hit the gym. And I am not asking you go to gym and start training randomly with a traditional work out routine, but a special dedicated training plan helping you boost your test levels in a week.

Strength training plan–The compound exercises

Studies have proven that doing compound and multi joint exercises, have a drastic effect on male test levels. What are these compound exercises?

Squats

Squats are the grand daddy of all exercises. And what we don't know is that performing squats can not only add insane amount of muscle mass in no time but also increase your sex drive. Squats will give you the hormonal boost, which you need to get your test levels up in a week.

Also note, quads (thighs) it's thc biggest muscle in our body, and squats is the only exercise which gives your quads a complete work out. Plus it engages the whole body from your core, hips, to your lower back by keeping it together.

Remember you need to work on bigger muscle groups, and engage whole body movement to increase your test levels. A recent study published in the journal of sports medicine states that any resistance exercise, which involves large muscle groups would have a drastic and positive effect on the test levels.

Deadlifts

Another compound movement, deadlifts is one of the most effective exercise to strengthen your muscles. It has been stated in many researches that a heavy deadlift session can have a great positive effect on man's sex drive. So you need to perform deadlifts.

Bench press

This is also a multi joint compound exercise, which will engage your complete body some way or the other. Remember, you are not doing these exercises to build muscles, because muscles cannot be build in a week, you are doing these to boost or spike your test levels.

Sprints

High interval intensity training (HIIT) is what I would call it. A good sprinting session will use all your energy and at the same time will give you a test spike. Remember you can't do regular boring cardio. As I said, this is a week program, for your immediate test boost.

THE TRAINING SCHEDULE

Monday

Squats 6 sets, 6 reps each

Deadlifts, 6 sets, 6 reps each

Bench press, 6 sets, 6 reps each

Tuesday

1 min sprint 1 min rest

30 mins (15 mins sprinting 15 mins rest)

Wednesday

Rest

Thursday

Repeat Monday

Friday

Repeat Tuesday

Saturday

Repeat Monday

Sunday

Rest

Remember this program is meant to shock your body and give you the much-needed spike in your test levels.

Who can follow this one-week program?

Anyone who is looking to spike his or her test levels can do this program. Remember this will work as a good shock therapy for many breaking their mundane pattern of training.

Diet and Nutrition

Remember, we need to add certain food items, which are high in cholesterol, because testosterone is made up of cholesterol. But this will only be for a week.

Again I will ask you to eat certain food items, which you typically won't eat on a muscle gain program but a quick fix to jumpstart your test levels in a week.

But you would question, on the certain side effect of eating cholesterol rich food items. Well as I said, this will be only for a week, but I will still suggest speak with your doctor before taking this one week program, especially if you have high cholesterol

Coconut

We need to add good fats to increase our test levels and coconut is one of them, a healthy saturated fat source. Coconut will help your body to produce cholesterol naturally, and at the same time keep your weight under check.

Broccoli, asparagus and cauliflower

You need to add these three food items in your meal, since these items are anti estrogen and will help your body increase the test levels naturally.

Tuna

Personally I am not a big fan of tuna, but this is something I had to put into this food plan simply because of its nutritional value especially vitamin D content. Vitamin D increases your test levels.

Beans

Beans are rich in zinc and vitamin D, and both helps in increasing the test levels. Focus more on kidney beans, as they are good for your heart as well.

Pomegranate

As per the research, consumption of pomegranate, especially the juice can improve the condition of impotent men by 55%. Now why don't we add that into our diet plan?

Honey

This you can use in your daily beverages. Did you know honey could improve the strength of your erection by 25%?

Garlic

This is a must to lower your stress hormone, cortisol. If we don't suppress this stress hormone cortisol, any of the test boosting foods won't work.

Diet schedule

- Breakfast–Oats and whole eggs (we need the yolk)
- Coffee/tea with honey 2 table spoon
- Pre lunch snack- pomegranate juice
- Lunch- Bowl of kidney beans with rice and salad including asparagus, broccoli and cauliflower
- Evening snack- Coconut water
- Dinner- Tuna/beans

SUPPLEMENTS

Ashwagandha

The traditional Indian herb ideally used to lower stress and anxiety levels. But there have been studies claiming its uses in increasing male test levels by over 40%.

When to use:

With your breakfast

Zinc

This is one supplement, which is highly underrated but works very well. ZMA, it is commonly called. It not only helps with stress free sleep, but also has the ability to maintain erections and healthy test levels.

When to use

20 mg before going to bed

L arginine

This is a surprising supplement to be featured here. But you would know its importance after 4 days. L arginine will help you increase the blood flow, which will eventually lead to better erection.

What has worked for me is 5 grams before working out. Because it's a vasodilator, it can be used a pre work out as well.

Vitamin D

The natural source of Vitamin D is sunshine. If you were to do sun bathing three times a week for fifteen minutes, you will see a change in the test levels. We usually underestimate the power of sun, but it has some great benefits. In summers, I wont recommend this.

Tribulus

This is an Indian herb, works on almost every Indian man. It is primarily used for male sexual wellness and well-being. In Hindi terms it is also called as Gokshura, available at any popular pharmacy.

Tribuls is one of the most cost effective supplements you will ever get your hands on. And this is by far the supplement which you can use yearlong.

ABOUT THE AUTHOR

Tarun Gill is India's leading fitness entrepreneur and an influencer with a following of more than 1 million.

He is also a founder of one of India's biggest fitness media digital platform, TG Talks.

He is a graduate from St. Stephens College, Masters in Journalism from Indian institute of Mass Communication and an MBA in marketing management.

After serving more than 5 fortune hundred companies including Metlife, HSBC, GE, IBM, Tarun took up fitness as a full time career, becoming India's first full time fitness Youtuber.

Tarun is also an Amazon bestselling fitness author and a Founder of TG Connect, India's only fitness social recognition platform endorsed by famous Bollywood a listers. With his reach and network, he was able to launch, India's first fitness TV show called the Indian Fitness League, IFL which was aired on DSport, a Premium Sports Channel by Discovery Sports in the year 2018.

Tarun Gill is India's leading fitness entrepreneur and an influencer with a following of more than 1 million.

He is also a founder of one of India's biggest fitness media digital platform, TG [illegible]

[illegible] Indian [illegible] management.

After spending more than 15 fortune [illegible] including Mobile [illegible]

[illegible]

[illegible] entrepreneurship [illegible] Bollywood a [illegible] with his coach and mentor. He was [illegible] India's [illegible] fitness TV show called the Indian Fitness League, IFL which was aired [illegible] Premium [illegible] Channel by Discovery Sports in the year 2016.